Rachel's
IRISH FAMILY FOOD

Rachel's
IRISH FAMILY FOOD

120 classic recipes from my home to yours

RACHEL ALLEN

Contents

Introduction

This is a cookbook I have always wanted to write. It's a collection of my very best family recipes, seriously comforting and nourishing food, all inspired by both traditional and modern Irish cooking. In Ireland we have fabulous ingredient-led dishes that make the most of the incredible produce from our farms and fish and seafood from our coast. These are my favorite recipes to cook for my family, the ones I turn to again and again. Whether or not you're familiar with Irish food, I'm sure you'll love this introduction to our country's culinary culture.

Irish food has a rich history and tradition. Of course, our love for the potato is well known and very real, but with recipes such as colcannon, Irish stew, and our wonderful soda bread, there are so many distinctively Irish dishes that make our food ideal for home-cooked meals—wherever in the world you might live. I grew up in Dublin and my mum was a very good cook. She would often have casseroles gently bubbling in the oven, filling the kitchen with their alluring aromas to make my sister and me ever more impatiently hungry.

My own relationship with cooking started with baking. My sister, mother, and I would often bake together, making biscuits (cookies) or cakes. I loved the whole process, from the messy mixing to the mysterious rise behind the oven door. It was at the age of eighteen that my interest in cooking became a passion and eventually an obsession. I traveled down to East Cork to study at the famous Ballymaloe Cookery School, which at the time had been going for six years, and at which I still teach to this day. It was at the cooking school that I met its founder, Darina Allen, who would eventually become my mother-in-law! I also met her mother-in-law, Myrtle Allen, the matriarch of Irish food who had founded the Ballymaloe House Restaurant and guest house all the way back in 1964.

On my first day at the cooking school I learned many of the principles that we still teach students today: That the best food comes from the best ingredients and that means carefully grown crops and lovingly raised animals. The school sits in the middle of an organic farm from which we get the students' cooking ingredients. It opened my eyes to how much more important proper produce is than complicated or long-winded recipes.

This is echoed by our impressive and still rapidly expanding modern Irish food culture. Ours is not a history of elaborate multilayered dishes. Irish food is about local produce. The greenest grass in the world feeds the happiest cows, which in turn produce the most beautiful butter and cheeses. We have teams of small dedicated farmers who put their efforts into growing delectable crops and our cold water creates the sweetest seafood. With ingredients like this, I think it's important not to dress up the food too much, to let their flavors take center stage. Whether you and your family live in New York or Minnesota, Cape Town or Brisbane, I'd always encourage you to buy from your local producers and farmers' markets, keep your home cooking simple and make the most of the fantastic ingredients the fertile plains of America or stunning coast of Australia have to offer. This book is filled with simple and easily achievable dishes that I love to cook and, perhaps most importantly, that I love to eat!

The recipes range from light suppers for a summer's evening to big hearty casseroles for when the wind is blowing and the rain is lashing down. There are everyday dinners for school nights when you've been at work all day, as well as slightly more involved recipes when you want to make something a little more special. All the recipes are easy to follow and not at all difficult to execute.

I've also included four passages about each of the different provinces in Ireland, with information about the food as well as the people, their history, and folklore. Irish culture is ancient but alive and vibrant, with food a fundamental piece of it. Part of our history is the waves of emigration and there are so many people—especially in the US—who have Irish ancestry and heritage. I hope that through our food you can connect both to the history of Ireland and to the wonderful country that it still is today.

Soups and light meals

These are the sorts of dishes I like to serve as a casual supper or a light lunch. They are versatile recipes and not too filling. A soup, for example, can easily feed a family if accompanied by lots of delicious crusty bread. Probably due in no small part to our blustery and bracing weather, there is a real tradition of warming soups in Ireland. It might be a nourishing broth such as the West Cork Broth with Gubbeen Bacon (page 43) or a rich and creamy comforting soup like the two different chowder recipes in this chapter.

Lots of the recipes in this chapter would also work really well as an appetizer for a larger meal. Asparagus with Hollandaise Sauce (page 12) is one of my absolute favorites when made with perfect Irish butter from our greenest pastures. It makes the most divine supper on its own, but if you're having guests over, then a few asparagus spears cooked this way is a lovely way to begin a meal. The same is true of the wonderfully Irish combination of fresh oysters with a glass of Guinness (page 25).

Asparagus on toast with hollandaise sauce

Vegetarian

Serves 4

Preparation time: 5 minutes

Cooking time: 20 minutes

16 to 20 asparagus spears

Good pinch of salt

A few slices of Brown Soda Bread (page 227)

Butter

Hollandaise sauce (see below)

Asparagus has to be my favorite vegetable. The exquisitely flavored bright green spears have a season that is always sadly short. Ireland has perfect growing conditions to produce some of the best asparagus I've ever tasted. There are lots of different ways of cooking and serving asparagus, but to me this is the very best: simply boiled in salted water and served on Brown Soda Bread (page 227) with butter and lashings of hollandaise sauce.

Snap off the tough woody end of each asparagus stalk and discard. Fill a large saucepan to a depth of 1½ to 2½ inches (4–6cm) with water, add the salt, and bring to a boil. Tip in the asparagus and cook in the boiling water for 4 to 8 minutes, until tender when pierced with a sharp knife. Drain immediately.

While the asparagus is cooking, toast the bread, then spread with the butter and remove the crusts, if you wish. For each person, place a piece of toast on a warmed plate, put 4 to 5 asparagus spears on top, and spoon over a little hollandaise sauce.

Hollandaise sauce

Vegetarian

Makes ⅓ cup (75 ml)

Preparation time: 5 minutes

Cooking time: 5 minutes

1 egg yolk

1 tablespoon cold water

4 tablespoons (50g) butter, diced

Freshly squeezed lemon juice

Salt and freshly ground black pepper

Place a heatproof bowl over a saucepan of simmering water over medium heat. (The water must not boil to avoid heating the sauce so much it scrambles or curdles; take the pan off the heat every so often.) Add the egg yolk and cold water. Whisking all the time, gradually add the butter, a few pieces at a time, until each addition has melted and emulsified before adding the next.

Once all the butter has been incorporated, season to taste with lemon juice and salt and pepper, if necessary. Remove from the heat and serve immediately or leave to sit over the warm water until you're ready to serve.

Artichokes with melted butter

Vegetarian

Serves 6

Preparation time: 5 minutes

Cooking time: 30 minutes

6 globe artichokes

Salt

White wine vinegar

¾ cup (175g) butter

Juice of ½ lemon, freshly squeezed, plus extra for dipping

Globe artichokes have been grown in the gardens of Irish country houses such as Ballymaloe for years. They make a beautiful plant, tall and proud, but it is their bright purple thistle-like flower heads that cooks prize. This is my favorite way of serving them. No olive oil here, only simply boiled artichokes and perfect Irish butter. I love the quiet methodical way one eats artichokes. To eat them, pull away each leaf from the artichoke, dip in the butter, then put the leaf in your mouth and scrape off the flesh from the base with your teeth. Discard that leaf and pick another. Eventually you'll get down to the yellow choke: Scrape this off and discard to reveal the tender and juicy heart.

Just before cooking, trim the base of the artichokes so they will sit steadily on the plate. Dip the cut end in lemon juice to prevent it from discoloring.

Fill a saucepan large enough to hold all of the artichokes three-quarters full with water. Add 2 teaspoons salt and 2 teaspoons white wine vinegar for every quart (liter) of water. Bring to a boil over high heat.

Carefully add the artichokes (they should be completely covered with water). Bring back to a boil, then decrease the heat to medium and simmer for about 25 minutes, until the larger leaves at the base of the plant come away easily if you pull on them. If they don't, then continue to cook for another 5 to 10 minutes. When cooked, remove the artichokes from the water and drain upside down on a plate.

While the artichokes cook, heat the butter in a saucepan over medium-low heat just until melted, then stir in the lemon juice, transfer to a few serving bowls, and set aside.

To serve, remove the tough outer leaves and discard. Place each artichoke, while still warm, onto a serving plate. Either give each person their own serving bowl of butter or have the bowls within easy reach.

Dublin bay prawns with mayonnaise

Serves 4 to 6

Preparation time: 5 minutes

Cooking time: 5 minutes

5 quarts (4.8l) water

4 tablespoons salt

2¼ pounds (1kg) Dublin bay prawns with heads on, or any large shrimp

Mayonnaise (see below), to serve

Langoustines are known as Dublin bay prawns in Ireland. Their divine sweetness is a result of our cold waters, and I love to eat them simply, with just a little mayonnaise, either plain or with a few herbs stirred through.

Fill a large saucepan with the water, add the salt, and bring to a boil over high heat. When the water is at a good rolling boil, add the prawns. Return the water to a boil and cook for 2 to 3 minutes, depending on their size. The best way to tell when prawns are cooked is to take one from the pan once they rise to the top of the water, after a minute or so of boiling. If it is opaque and firm all the way through, then they are ready to drain.

As soon as the prawns are cooked, drain and lay them out to cool on flat trays to keep them from cooking any further.

Serve at room temperature with a bowl of mayonnaise on the side.

Mayonnaise

Vegetarian

Makes 1¼ cups (300ml)

Preparation time: 5 minutes

2 egg yolks

Pinch of salt

1 teaspoon Dijon mustard

2 teaspoons white wine vinegar

¾ cup (200ml) sunflower oil

1 tablespoon plus 2 teaspoons (25ml) extra virgin olive oil

Freshly ground black pepper

2 tablespoons chopped fresh herbs (chives, dill, fennel) (optional)

Put the egg yolks in a bowl and mix in the salt, mustard, and vinegar.

Mix the sunflower oil and the extra virgin olive oil in a pitcher.

Very gradually, whisking all the time (either by hand or using handheld electric beater), slowly pour the oil into the bowl in a very thin stream. You should see the mixture start to thicken. Keep whisking and adding the oil slowly until it has all been incorporated. Season with pepper and more salt to taste. Stir in the chopped herbs (if using).

Ivan Allen's dressed crab

Serves 6

Preparation time: 15 minutes
(plus 45 minutes to prep crabs)

Cooking time: 20 minutes
(plus 40 minutes to cook crabs)

1 pound (425g) meat from 3 to
4 cooked fresh large crabs,
reserving the crab shells

4½ cups (200g) soft white bread
crumbs

⅔ cup (150ml) Basic White Sauce
(page 114)

2 tablespoons Tomato Relish
(page 20)

2 teaspoons white wine vinegar

1 teaspoon Dijon mustard, or a
generous pinch of dry mustard
powder

5 tablespoons (75g) butter, melted

Salt and freshly ground black
pepper

FOR THE TOMATO AND BASIL SALAD

8 vine-ripened tomatoes (using one
variety or a mixture)

Salt and freshly ground black
pepper

Pinch of sugar

Juice from a good squeeze of lemon

2 to 3 tablespoons extra virgin
olive oil

Small handful of basil leaves, larger
leaves torn

Ivan Allen was Isaac's grandfather, and this is his recipe. I remember him coming into the kitchens at Ballymaloe and checking the dressed crab whenever it was on the menu to ensure it was just right. If you are using brown crabs, try to find whole crabs so that you can use both the white and flavorful brown meat. I've given instructions for cooking a crab from scratch, but if you can't get hold of a whole crab, you can use ready-cooked fresh or frozen crabmeat instead. For serving you will need two or three crab shells or six 1-cup (250ml) ramekins or small dishes.

Preheat the oven to 350°F (180°C/Gas mark 4). If you plan to serve from the crab shells, scrub them clean, dry well, and arrange upside down on a baking sheet. Alternatively, place six 1-cup (250ml) ramekins or small dishes on the baking sheet.

In a large bowl, mix together the crabmeat, just over three-quarters of the bread crumbs, the white sauce, relish, vinegar, mustard, and 2 tablespoons of the melted butter; season to taste with salt and pepper. Spoon the mixture into the crab shells or ramekins. In a separate bowl, toss together the remaining bread crumbs with the remaining 3 tablespoons butter and sprinkle over the crab mixture.

Bake for 15 to 20 minutes, until heated through and browned on top. Briefly place under a preheated broiler (grill), if necessary, to crisp up the crumbs.

In the meantime, prepare the salad. Cut the tomatoes into quarters or ½-inch (1cm) slices. Spread out in a single layer on a large flat plate and season to taste with salt, pepper, and sugar. Drizzle over the lemon juice, then the extra virgin olive oil; scatter the basil leaves over. Toss together gently.

Serve the baked crab with the tomato salad and some fresh crusty bread on the side.

How to cook a crab

First place the crab in the freezer for a couple of hours so that it is unconscious before boiling. Place the frozen crab in a large saucepan, cover with warm water, add 1 tablespoon of salt for every 5 cups (1.2 liters) of water and bring to a boil. Simmer over medium heat for

recipe continues overleaf

20 minutes for every pound (450g). Pour off about two-thirds of the water, cover with a lid, and continue to cook for another 6 minutes. To see if the crab is cooked, gently shake it quite close to your ear; you shouldn't hear liquid splashing around. If you do hear water, the crab isn't quite cooked and will need another few minutes. Remove the crab from the water and allow to cool.

To remove the meat, first remove the large claws and crack these (using a heavy weight or nut crackers), then extract every bit of meat using the handle of a teaspoon. Turn the body of the crab upside down and pull out the center portion. Discard the gills, known as "dead man's fingers," each about 1½ inches (4cm) long. Scoop out all the lovely brown meat from the body and add it to the meat from the claws. The meat can be used immediately or frozen for future use. Retain the shell if making dressed crab, otherwise discard.

Tomato relish

Vegetarian

Makes 1 half-pint (300ml) jar

Preparation time: 5 minutes

Cooking time: 2 hours

1 (14-ounce/400g) can diced tomatoes

1 onion, finely chopped

¾ cup (200ml) white wine vinegar

⅔ cup (130g) superfine (caster) or
   granulated sugar

⅔ cup (100g) golden raisins
   (sultanas) or raisins

4 tablespoons water

1 teaspoon whole-grain mustard

1 teaspoon tomato paste (purée)

½ teaspoon ground cumin

½ teaspoon ground coriander

Pinch of ground cloves

A really useful relish recipe, this is my version of Ballymaloe Country Relish, which is sold all over Ireland and in some stores in the U.S. It works with many different foods, from cold meats and sausages to cheese sandwiches and dressed crab.

Combine all ingredients in a saucepan over low heat. Bring to a simmer and continue to cook on a low simmer, stirring occasionally, for about 1½ hours, until a slightly reduced chunky consistency. Use immediately or store in a covered jar in the refrigerator for up to 2 months.

Mussels with garlic and bread crumbs

Serves 4 to 6

Preparation time: 10 minutes

Cooking time: 10 minutes

2 pounds (900g) mussels in their shells, scrubbed clean

4 tablespoons (50g) butter

1 cup (50g) fresh white bread crumbs (see tip below)

1 large clove garlic, crushed or grated

1 tablespoon chopped fresh parsley

These are a retro favorite, beloved of Irish restaurants in the eighties. When done right, they're absolutely fantastic: crisp crunchy bread crumbs atop plump mussels. Mussels, one of the least expensive of shellfish, grow freely on our shores and have long fed the people of the coast. They're such good value, and I love that they're so quick to cook. Serve with bread or toast to mop up all the juices.

Check over the mussels and, if any are open, give them a tap; if they don't close, discard them. Put the tightly shut mussels with just 1 tablespoon of water in a large saucepan over low heat and cover with the lid. They will open in the steam. If you catch them when they are just opening, they will be delicious and juicy, so don't overcook them. Remove the mussels from the pan (keeping any juices for a fish soup, pie, stew, or even to mix with mayonnaise served with shellfish such as shrimp). Discard any cooked mussels with unopened shells.

Discard half a shell from each mussel and pull out the beard—the little fibrous tuft— from the straight side of each mussel.

Melt the butter in a medium saucepan over medium-low heat. Add the bread crumbs, garlic, and parsley and mix together. With a spoon, firmly pack the bread crumb mixture on top of each mussel. Place the mussels, crumb side up, in a single layer on ovenproof plates or gratin dishes. (These can be prepared up to 24 hours in advance.) When you are ready to eat, pop them under a preheated broiler (grill) until golden, crunchy, and bubbly, 1 to 2 minutes.

Variations
While it isn't classically Irish, sometimes I feel like adding a bit more zip to this recipe, so in place of the parsley, I add 1 tablespoon chopped fresh cilantro (coriander) together with one-quarter to one-half of a fresh red chile, seeded and chopped. Or you could try adding some grated lemon zest to the crumbs.

Rachel's tip
To make bread crumbs, place slices of white bread (with or without the crusts) in a food processor, and whiz until you have crumbs, about 20 seconds.

Oysters with Guinness

Serves 4

Preparation time: 30 minutes

24 oysters (opened in their shells)

A glass of Guinness each, to serve

Lemon wedges, pepper, or Tabasco
sauce, to serve (optional)

Once considered a food for the peasants, oysters are now a prized delicacy. There is nothing quite like the salty, creamy flesh that tastes so much of the sea. In Ireland, oysters are always shucked to order, and they are celebrated at oyster festivals across the country with shucking competitions and various oyster-based events.

Oysters need little accompaniment; some people like a few grinds of pepper or drops of Tabasco or lemon. It's up to you, though I like the pure unadulterated oyster flavor and have mine on their own. Stout and oysters go particularly well with each other, and the two served together is a quintessentially Irish dish. For a more celebratory drink, you could make Black Velvets, which are a classic Irish drink made by adding two parts stout to one part Champagne. Both my husband Isaac and I adore Black Velvets whether with oysters or without, and we served them at midnight at our wedding.

How to open an oyster

It is best to use an oyster knife, which is designed for the purpose and will make your life much easier (and safer). If you don't have an oyster knife, you can use a thin chisel, but do not attempt to open oysters with any knife that has a bendy blade.

Fold a kitchen towel lengthwise and wrap it around your hand once or twice to protect it. Place the oyster on the remaining edge of the towel, with the flatter side of the oyster facing up. You will see a slight crevice where the shells meet at the narrow end.

Take your oyster knife (or thin clean chisel) and insert the blade into the crevice while holding the opposite end steady with your wrapped hand. Press and turn the knife, levering upwards. Once the shell pops open, insert a clean knife just under the top shell to cut the oyster away; it will suddenly become free.

Cut the membrane where the oyster is attached to the shell and remove the oyster altogether or replace it on the shell, discarding any bits of broken shell. Serve immediately, if possible, or store refrigerated in a sealed container until serving.

Smoked mackerel pâté

Serves 4 to 6

Preparation time: 15 minutes

Cooking time: 15 to 20 minutes

1 large fillet smoked mackerel
(about 3½ ounces/100g)

⅓ cup (75g) cream cheese, softened

⅓ cup (75g) crème fraîche or sour
cream

Juice of ½ lemon

Salt and freshly ground black
pepper

This is one of my favorite quick recipes, as impressive as it is quick to put together. I love having some of this in my fridge for a snack or a packed lunch, and it will keep there for a week. The better the smoked mackerel you use the better your pâté will be. I sometimes serve this on slices of Brown Soda Bread (page 227) with Cucumber Pickle (page 133). For a family meal I like to serve this pâté as an appetizer, in a bowl in the center of the table with lots of crusty bread or toast to go around. That way everyone can dig in while the rest of the meal is being prepared.

In a food processor, whiz the smoked mackerel. Add the cream cheese and the crème fraîche or sour cream and whiz just until smooth. Empty into a bowl and fold in the lemon juice, salt, and pepper to taste.

Chicken livers with bacon and sage

Serves 2 to 4

Preparation time: 10 minutes

Cooking time: 15 minutes

2 tablespoons extra virgin olive oil

5 ounces (150g) bacon, cut into
¾-inch (2cm) pieces

1 clove garlic, sliced

10 ounces (300g) chicken livers,
green parts removed

Salt and freshly ground black
pepper

1 to 2 tablespoons chopped fresh
sage

2 tablespoons marsala, port, or
brandy

4 tablespoons light (single) cream
(optional)

I adore chicken livers for their soft texture and rich flavor. Chicken livers are less popular in Ireland than they used to be, when people would make sure to eat every part of the animal. Chicken livers and crispy bacon is a classic combination and makes a divine appetizer with some crusty bread, or serve as a supper with Creamy Mashed Potato (page 166).

Add 1 tablespoon of the olive oil to a frying pan over medium heat. Add the bacon and fry for a few minutes until golden, then transfer onto paper towels to drain, then set aside.

Add the remaining 1 tablespoon of olive oil and the garlic and fry for 1 to 2 minutes, until slightly gold.

Add the chicken livers, season with salt and pepper, and cook the livers for 2 to 3 minutes on each side, until they're browned on the outside but still a little pink in the middle.

Add the reserved bacon, sage, and marsala. Increase the heat and bubble for just 30 seconds (be careful as the alcohol may flame), then remove from the heat.

If you'd like a creamier dish, leave the pan over high heat, add the cream, and allow it to bubble for 30 seconds or so.

Season to taste and serve immediately.

Chicken livers with onions

Serves 2

Preparation time: 10 minutes

Cooking time: 30 minutes

2 tablespoons (25g) butter

2 onions, thinly sliced

10 ounces (300g) chicken livers

Salt and freshly ground black pepper

2 tablespoons dry sherry

½ cup (100ml) chicken stock (page 35) or vegetable stock (page 34)

The Irish have always believed it is important to eat the whole animal. Livers or kidneys are often served alongside our beloved potatoes, which may be simply boiled or in a creamy mash. This is a more modern version of a dish my grandmother used to make a lot. The dry sherry gives the dish real depth; you could also use brandy, port, or even white wine. If you have time, make some Creamy Mashed Potato (page 166) to accompany them. Otherwise make sure to mop up every last drop with some good crusty bread.

Melt 1 tablespoon of the butter in a frying pan over medium-high heat and, when foaming, add the onions. Fry, stirring occasionally, for 15 to 20 minutes, until the onions are completely soft and golden. Tip the onions onto a plate and set aside.

Season the chicken livers with salt and pepper. Melt the remaining 1 tablespoon butter in the pan over medium-high heat. When the butter starts to foam, add the chicken livers and cook for 2 to 4 minutes on each side, until browned on the outside but still a little pink in the middle.

Add the sherry and allow it to bubble for 30 seconds. Add the cooked onions and stock. Stir together, bring to a boil, then decrease the heat to medium-low and cook for 1 to 2 minutes, until the stock has slightly reduced. Serve immediately.

Field mushroom soup

Vegetarian (if using vegetable stock)

Serves 6

Preparation time: 10 minutes

Cooking time: 40 minutes

2 tablespoons (25g) butter

1 onion, finely chopped

2 cloves garlic, finely chopped

12 ounces (350g) large flat
    field mushrooms or button
    mushrooms, quartered

1 tablespoon chopped fresh thyme

Salt and freshly ground black
    pepper

2½ cups (600ml) chicken stock
    (page 35) or vegetable stock
    (page 34)

⅔ cup (150ml) heavy or whipping
    cream (double or regular) cream

1 tablespoon finely chopped fresh
    chives

Mushroom soup is an easy family favorite, rich and velvety with a lovely texture because it isn't puréed. From the mountains of Wicklow to the woodlands of Kerry, we have an abundance of great wild and farmed mushrooms in Ireland. I use large flat field mushrooms (called meadow mushrooms in North America) when I can because they have a better flavor than the smaller button mushrooms.

Melt the butter in a large saucepan over medium heat. Add the onion and garlic and cook for 8 to 10 minutes, until softened and slightly golden.

Finely chop the mushrooms in the food processor or by hand and add the mushrooms to the saucepan along with the thyme. Place over medium-low heat, cover, and cook for about 5 minutes or until softened. Season with salt and pepper. Pour in the stock and bring slowly to a boil; then decrease the heat and simmer gently for 25 minutes.

Pour in the cream and simmer gently for a few minutes, then stir in the chives and serve immediately.

Vegetable stock

Vegetarian

Makes about 8½ cups (2l)

Preparation time: 10 minutes

Cooking time: 1 hour

2 onions, coarsely chopped

2 leeks, trimmed and coarsely chopped

3 celery stalks, trimmed and coarsely chopped

3 carrots, coarsely chopped

½ fennel bulb, coarsely chopped

Bunch of parsley stems

1 small sprig of rosemary

1 sprig of thyme

Water

A really useful stock, perfect for vegetarians or when you don't want a meaty flavor in your dish.

Combine the onions, leeks, celery, carrots, fennel, parsley, rosemary, and thyme in a large saucepan. Add enough cold water to cover the ingredients by about 4 inches (10cm) and bring to a simmer. Continue to simmer for an hour, then strain the liquid and discard the vegetables.

Chicken stock

Makes about 8½ cups (2l)

Preparation time: 5 minutes

Cooking time: 2 hours

1 chicken carcass (either raw or cooked)

1 onion, unpeeled and halved, or 1 leek, split and halved

1 to 2 carrots, halved lengthwise

1 celery stalk

1 small bay leaf

1 sprig of parsley

1 sprig of thyme

4 peppercorns

12⅔ cups (3l) water

Salt and freshly ground black pepper

Chicken stock is invaluable, forming the basis for so many stews, sauces, and soups. Homemade chicken stock, with its intense, fresh flavor, is best of all. Indeed, making stock is a very good way of using up ingredients that might otherwise be thrown away—onion peel, carrot and celery trimmings and, of course, chicken bones. Get into the habit of making stock whenever you have a chicken carcass on hand—whether cooked or raw. If you're not using the stock straight away, it will store in the fridge for 2 to 3 days, or you can pour it into several small containers to freeze.

Combine the chicken carcass, onion, carrots, celery, bay leaf, parsley, thyme, and peppercorns in a large saucepan. Add the water and bring to a boil. Decrease the heat and simmer over medium heat, covered but with a wooden spoon between the lid and the pan to allow the steam to escape, for about 2 hours, until you have a well-flavored stock.

Strain the stock through a fine sieve into a large bowl or pitcher, discarding the bits in the sieve. Allow to cool, skimming off any fat from the surface of the stock as it cools.

Ballycotton fish chowder

Serves 4

Preparation time: 15 minutes

Cooking time: 15 to 20 minutes

Extra virgin olive oil

3 ounces (100g) bacon, cut into
⅜-inch (1cm) dice

1 small onion, chopped

Salt and freshly ground black
pepper

6 ounces (175g) potatoes, peeled
and cut into ⅜-inch (1cm) cubes

2 cups (500ml) chicken stock
(page 35)

1½ cups (350ml) milk

Pinch of cayenne pepper

8 ounces (200g) fish fillets (mixture
of salmon and a white fish, such
as pollock, haddock, or cod) cut
into ¾- to 1-inch (2–3cm) chunks

3 ounces (100g) smoked haddock or
smoked salmon, cut into ¾-inch
(2cm) pieces

1 tablespoon chopped fresh chives

1 tablespoon chopped fresh parsley

Ballycotton is our local fishing village, and nearly all the fish we eat and cook here at the Ballymaloe Cookery School comes from there. Ireland's long coastline gives a glorious abundance of the very best fish, and chowder is a much loved staple on pub, café, and restaurant menus throughout the coast. The best of the local fish goes into this rich and creamy soup. I always make chowder using some smoked fish because I love the way that smokiness flavors the whole bowl. You can also add some whole mussels in their shells (be sure to discard any that remain closed after cooking).

Serve with Brown Soda Bread (page 227), Wholemeal Honey Bread (page 233), or Brown Yeast Bread (page 230).

Pour a small drizzle of olive oil into a large saucepan over medium heat. When the oil is hot, tip in the bacon. Fry for 4 to 5 minutes, stirring occasionally, until all the fat has rendered and the bacon is crispy and golden brown.

Add the onion, season with salt and pepper (bearing in mind that the bacon is quite salty), and cook for another 5 minutes. Then add the potatoes with the stock, milk, and cayenne.

Bring to a boil, decrease the heat, and simmer for 3 minutes, or until the cubes of potato are half cooked. Add the fish and gently simmer for another 3 to 4 minutes, until the fish is opaque and the potatoes are tender. Season with salt and pepper to taste, stir in the chopped herbs, and serve.

Molly Malone's cockle and mussel chowder

Serves 4 to 6

Preparation time: 10 minutes

Cooking time: 20 minutes

2 tablespoons sunflower oil

4 ounces (110g) smoked bacon, diced

2 tablespoons (25g) butter

4 ounces (110g) leek, trimmed and very finely diced

4 ounces (110g) carrot, very finely diced

10 ounces (275g) potato (about 1 medium), peeled and finely diced

2¼ pounds (1kg) mixed cockles and mussels

1¼ cups (300ml) dry white wine

¾ cup (200ml) milk

¾ cup (200ml) light (single) or heavy (double) cream

Salt and freshly ground black pepper

4 tablespoons coarsely chopped fresh parsley

Molly Malone was a beautiful girl who sold cockles and mussels and died tragically of a fever while still young, or so the song goes. Molly may not have been a real girl, but since at least the seventeenth century, there have been fishmongers on the streets of Dublin who sell "Cockles and Mussels, alive, alive, oh!"

Cockles, with their distinctive flavor and lovely curved shell, are traditionally eaten in Ireland with Oatcakes (page 248). If you can only find mussels, this chowder will be just as good.

Serve either as a substantial appetizer or with chunks of crusty bread as a meal in its own right.

Heat the sunflower oil in a saucepan over medium-high heat. Add the bacon and sauté for about 1 minute, until crisp and golden. Add the butter in the pan and melt. Then add the leek, carrot, and potato. Reduce the heat to low and sauté gently for 4 to 5 minutes, until soft but not browned.

Meanwhile, prepare the cockles and mussels. Scrub the shells clean and discard any that remain open when you tap them against a hard surface. Remove the beard—the little fibrous tuft—from each mussel. Bring the wine to a boil in a large saucepan and add the cockles and mussels. Cover with a tight-fitting lid and cook for 3 to 4 minutes, shaking the pan occasionally, until the shells have opened.

Remove from the heat, drain the shellfish in a colander, reserving the cooking juices, and discard any shells that remain closed. Return the shellfish to the empty pan to keep warm. Place a fine sieve over a measuring cup and strain the cooking liquid. You should have at least 2½ cups (600ml); if not, add water to make up that quantity.

Add the pan juices and the milk to the bacon and vegetable mixture and bring to a boil. Decrease the heat and simmer for 6 to 8 minutes, until the potato is tender. Add the cream and simmer for another 2 to 3 minutes, until the soup is reduced and thickened slightly. Season with salt and pepper.

Meanwhile, remove half of the cockles and mussels from their shells and add them with the remaining cockles and mussels still in their shells to the chowder. Stir in the parsley and serve at once.

West Cork broth with Gubbeen bacon

Serves 6

Preparation time: 15 minutes

Cooking time: 25 minutes

- 8 ounces (250g) unsmoked, unsliced Gubbeen bacon (rind removed) or pancetta, cut into ⅜-inch (1cm) cubes
- 2 tablespoons olive or sunflower oil
- 5 ounces (150g) potatoes, peeled and cut into ¼-inch (5mm) dice
- 1 medium onion, finely chopped
- 2 celery stalks, finely chopped
- 2 cloves garlic, crushed or finely grated
- 1 pound (450g) tomatoes, peeled and diced, or 1 (14-ounce/400g) can chopped tomatoes
- Salt and freshly ground black pepper
- 1 teaspoon sugar
- 3½ cups (850ml) chicken stock (page 35)
- ¾ cup (50g) finely shredded kale or savoy cabbage
- 2 tablespoons chopped fresh flat-leaf parsley

This is a comforting, restorative broth—warming and nourishing in equal measure. It uses unsliced bacon, which is sadly becoming increasingly uncommon in many places outside of Ireland. It works so well in this dish, because the bacon is cut into cubes that have just the right amount of juicy meatiness. It uses unsmoked bacon, which in Ireland means asking your butcher for "green" bacon. If you can't find unsmoked bacon, use pancetta.

I like to use Gubbeen bacon; their farm in West Cork has deliciously happy pigs, and they also make one of my favorite Irish cheeses.

Bring a saucepan of water to a boil over high heat. Add the bacon cubes and cook for 1 minute. Drain and dry on paper towels.

Heat the oil in a large saucepan over medium heat. Add the bacon and fry for 3 to 5 minutes until crisp and golden; then add the potatoes, onion, celery, and garlic. Decrease the heat to medium-low, cover, and cook for 10 minutes, stirring occasionally. Stir in the tomatoes and season with salt, pepper, and sugar.

Add the stock and bring to a simmer. Cook for 5 minutes, stir in the kale, and simmer for a minute or so, until just tender. Taste for seasoning, sprinkle with the parsley, and serve.

Potato, leek, and smoked bacon soup

Serves 6

Preparation time: 15 minutes

Cooking time: 15 minutes

1 tablespoon sunflower or olive oil

4 slices (rashers) bacon, diced

2 tablespoons (25g) butter

1 onion, coarsely chopped

1 large leek, trimmed and diced

2 large potatoes (about 1 pound/450g in total)

Salt and freshly ground black pepper

5 cups (1.2l) chicken stock (page 35) or vegetable stock (page 34)

(page 35) ... (page 34)

FOR THE PARSLEY PESTO

½ ounce (15g) fresh flat-leaf parsley

1 clove garlic, coarsely chopped

1 tablespoon pine nuts, lightly toasted

1 tablespoon finely grated Parmesan cheese

4 tablespoons extra virgin olive oil, plus more if needed

Salt and freshly ground black pepper

A soup made from the kind of staples that few Irish kitchens are ever without, with the potatoes forming the basis of a rustic and substantial meal in a bowl. The smoky flavor from the bacon gives this soup magnificent depth. Parsley pesto is an updated version of what many years ago would have been simply chopped parsley. It speaks to a modern Ireland, with its international influences.

This soup is great served with Brown Soda Bread (page 227).

(page 227)

Heat the oil in a large saucepan over high heat, add the bacon, and sauté for about 1 minute, or until crisp and golden. Remove from the pan and drain on paper towels.

Decrease the heat a little and add the butter to the oil in the pan. When it has melted, add the onion, leek, and potatoes. Season with salt and pepper and cook gently for 8 to 10 minutes without browning. Pour in the stock and simmer gently for 5 minutes, or until the potatoes are completely cooked through.

Meanwhile, make the parsley pesto. Discard the stems from the parsley and put the leaves in a bowl with the garlic, pine nuts, Parmesan, and olive oil. Using a handheld blender, purée to a fairly smooth paste, adding a little more oil, if necessary, so that it is a thick but drizzling consistency. Alternatively, crush the parsley, garlic, and pine nuts using a mortar and pestle and stir in the Parmesan and olive oil. Season to taste with salt and pepper and set aside.

Purée the soup until smooth in a blender or using a handheld blender. Return to the pan and stir in all but 1 tablespoon of the reserved bacon pieces. Check the seasoning, adjusting if necessary, and heat for a minute more before serving.

Ladle the soup into warm bowls. Drizzle over the parsley pesto and scatter the remaining bacon pieces on top.

Rachel's tip

Collect the leek trimmings and parsley stems to add flavor when you are making stock.

Weeknights and everyday

Despite being around food all day, I never tire of cooking, and I cook for my family every day. Like everyone else, I find it useful to have a repertoire of dishes that I know really well and, importantly, that I know my children love eating. These are dishes that are easy to put together but never compromise on flavor. Many of these dishes are one-pot meals, such as the Kale and Bean Stew (page 49) and the Pork and Mushroom Pie (page 77). One-pot meals aren't only easier to cook, they really save on the clearing up!

This chapter includes a recipe for our beloved Irish Stew (page 81), which, as our national dish, has a grand tradition here. It is a deeply flavored dish made with lamb or mutton, and each county and even each family has its own version.

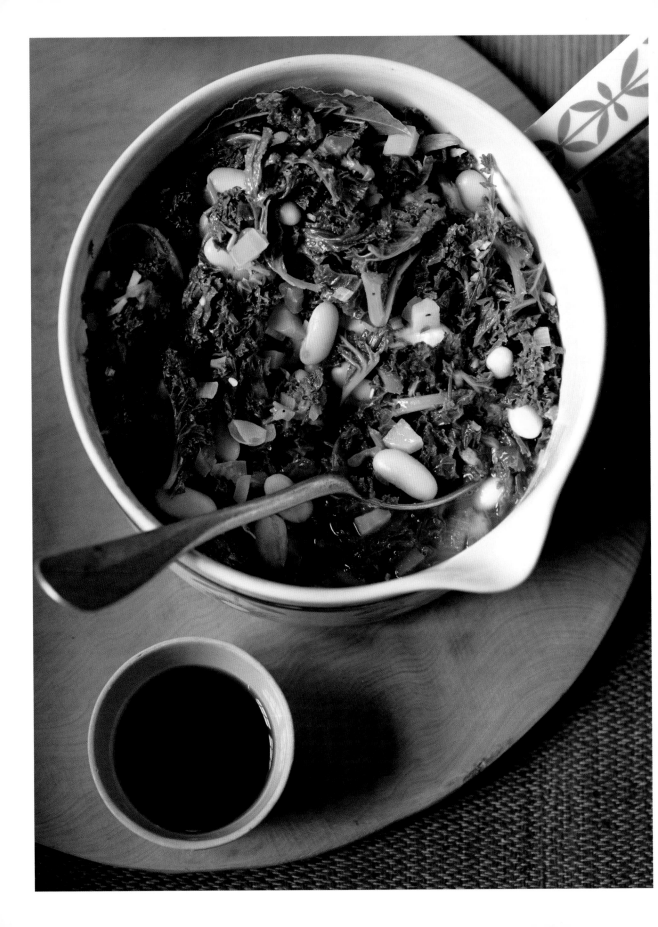

Kale and bean stew

Vegetarian (if using vegetable stock)

Serves 6 to 8

Preparation time: 20 minutes

Cooking time: 40 minutes

3 tablespoons extra virgin olive oil

1 carrot, chopped

1 celery stalk, trimmed and chopped

4 shallots, chopped

2 cloves garlic, finely chopped

Salt and freshly ground black pepper

1 cup (250ml) dry white wine

2 (14-ounce/400g) cans white beans, such as cannellini, butter, or haricot, drained and rinsed

3⅓ to 4½ cups (800ml–1l) chicken stock (page 35) or vegetable stock (page 34)

3 sprigs of thyme

1 bay leaf

7½ cups (500g) shredded kale leaves (stems and center ribs discarded)

1 tablespoon sherry vinegar

2 tablespoons fresh parsley, chopped, to serve

I love the deep nourishment that a bean and vegetable stew can provide in winter. Stews such as this one have been cooked in Ireland for a long time for their warmth and heartiness—perfect after a bracing walk in the wind and rain. Kale grows well in Ireland, and it is one of my favorite vegetables. There are a few different varieties. Curly kale is the most popular, but there is also red Russian kale and the fabulous Italian variety known as Tuscan kale, cavolo nero, or sometimes dinosaur kale due to its unusual bobbled appearance.

Heat the olive oil in a large saucepan over medium heat. Add the carrot, celery, shallots, and garlic. Season with salt and pepper and cook, stirring occasionally, for 10 to 12 minutes, until completely soft and lightly browned.

Add the white wine, bring to a simmer, and cook for about 5 minutes, or until the liquid is slightly reduced. Add the beans, 3⅓ cups (800ml) of the stock, the thyme, and bay leaf. Bring to a boil, decrease the heat to low, and simmer for about 15 minutes, until slightly reduced.

Add the kale and allow the stew to simmer for 3 to 5 minutes, until the kale is tender. Remove the thyme and bay leaf. If you would like a thinner stew, add a little more stock at this stage. Stir in the sherry vinegar, then taste for seasoning, and serve in bowls with a sprinkling of parsley.

Salad with beets, toasted hazelnuts, and Cashel Blue dressing

Vegetarian

Serves 4

Preparation time: 10 minutes

Cooking time: 30 to 45 minutes

---

4 small beets (beetroots) (about 5 ounces/150g in total)

⅓ cup (40g) hazelnuts, toasted and coarsely chopped

4 handfuls of salad greens

Finely grated zest of ½ lemon

About 20 slices Cucumber Pickle (page 113) (optional)

FOR THE DRESSING

½ cup (125ml) extra virgin olive oil

1 tablespoon freshly squeezed lemon juice

½ teaspoon honey

½ cup (75g) coarsely crumbled Cashel Blue cheese

Salt and freshly ground black pepper

Small, sweet summer beets make for a perfect simple salad. Their earthy sweetness works well when balanced with the creamy, salty taste of Cashel Blue cheese. This salad has a much needed crunch from toasted hazelnuts. If you desire, serve it with Cucumber Pickle (page 133).

First cook the beets. Wash the roots carefully under a cold tap. Do not scrub them—simply rub off any dirt with your fingers. You don't want to damage the skin or to cut off the tops or tails, otherwise the beets will "bleed" while cooking. Put the beets in a saucepan, cover with cold water, and bring to a simmer over medium heat. Cover and continue to simmer for 30 to 45 minutes, depending on the size and age of your beets. They are cooked when their skins rub off easily, and a knife can be inserted easily into the centers. Peel the beets by rubbing off and discarding the skins. Then cut each beet into eight wedges.

To make the dressing, mix together the olive oil, lemon juice, and honey in a bowl or jar, then add the blue cheese and taste, adding salt and pepper as needed.

Combine the beets and hazelnuts in a bowl, drizzle with three-quarters of the dressing, season, and toss.

Place the salad greens on one big serving plate or divide among individual plates and drizzle with the remaining dressing. Scatter the beets and the hazelnuts over the greens. Sprinkle over the grated lemon zest. If you desire, you can add four or five slices of cucumber pickle per person.

Leinster

Food in Ireland is characterized by a lavish abundance of natural, earthy produce. A cornucopia of nature's bounty is found in the fields and hedgerows of the counties of Leinster, a region where blue-gray mountains and romantic glens blend seamlessly with fertile lush valleys and majestic woodlands.

In the wild, blackberries, strawberries, sloes, damsons, crab apples, elderflowers, wood sorrel, hairy-leafed comfrey, spicy horseradish, and wild nettles are there for the picking. The acidic soils of the Wicklow uplands are the ideal place to find a small, purple fruit that grows on the prickly bilberry shrub. In Ireland we call these bilberries fraughans, and it's a word you'll hear in casual conversations at the height of the summer. The last Sunday in July heralds the Irish tradition of Domhnach na bhFraocháin, or Fraughan Sunday—the day these tasty berries, cousins of the cranberry, are at their ripest and ready to be gleaned. In times past, Irish families would climb the mountain ridges and fill their baskets with rotund fraughans. Their pickings were exported by boat and train to England, and this provided impoverished families with enough money to pay the grocery bill. Fraughans can be dried for use as "hedgerow currants," used in jams and jellies, or simply whipped off the bush, simmered in water and sugar, and then folded into some freshly whipped Irish cream to make the toothsome treat of fresh fraughan fool.

Dublin, the capital city of Ireland, is the home of Guinness, and the famous stout is made inside St. James' Gate using malting barley grown in fields throughout Ireland. Until a decade ago, the addition of Kilkenny-grown hops created the bitterness so characteristic of this Irish dry stout. Today, the craft brewing industry has flourished, and independent microbreweries, such as the Carlow Brewing Company and Kildare's Trouble Brewing, offer an artisanal alternative to Guinness and the like. The annual St. Patrick Day's parade in Dublin isn't the same without a slice of spicy porter cake, (see the recipe on page 198) a traditional fruit cake made all the more delicious with the addition of dark, smoky porter and served with a generous dollop of fresh Irish ice cream.

From the medieval fishing village of Slade, near Wexford's Hook Head, to Louth's Carlingford Lough, the chilly Irish Sea air blows across the length of Leinster's coastline. It's little wonder that coastal communities have long celebrated the sea's bounty. In August, the annual Carlingford Oyster Festival honors this salty fresh mollusk. It's a nod to Carlingford's Viking past when the fearless Nordic warriors feasted on this marine delicacy (see page 24 for ways in which you can enjoy this delicacy too). Fish for tea on Friday is a tradition still practiced in Ireland, and while salmon and sea trout remain kingly in the eyes of the Irish, delectable oily mackerel and luscious salted herrings (known as kippers) make frequent appearances on our plates.

Wild meat has somewhat faded from our collective consciousness, but there has been a recent resurgence of interest in it, and dishes such as wood pigeon pie, rabbit stew, roasted wild duck, and pheasant casserole can be enjoyed in many Irish eateries. Wild deer have long roamed the mountains of Leinster; remains of a medieval deer trap were recently discovered atop Carlow's Blackstairs Mountains, known in Irish as Na Staighrí Dubha. The prolific fallow deer population in Wicklow's Glencree Valley owes its presence to Anglo-Norman lords who introduced them into Ireland in the 12th century. Today, venison makes for a rich, sumptuous addition to traditional Irish stew. If you are more adventurous, try thinly sliced smoked venison, or juicy, iron-rich venison sausages, which are sold in Dublin's famous Temple Bar market each Saturday.

Fish cakes

Serves 4

Preparation time: 10 minutes

Cooking time: 25 minutes

1⅓ pounds (600g) baking or russet (floury) potatoes

Salt and freshly ground black pepper

14 ounces (400g) skinned white fish, such as cod, haddock, or hake

10 tablespoons (150g) butter, diced

4 tablespoons white wine

Juice of ¼ lemon

5 ounces (150g) button mushrooms, sliced

7 ounces (200g) cooked and peeled shrimp or small prawns (chop large shrimp)

2 egg yolks

1 tablespoon Dijon mustard

4 tablespoons finely chopped herbs, such as parsley, tarragon, dill, or chives (either one herb or a mixture)

3 to 4 tablespoons extra virgin olive oil

Salad greens and lemon wedges, to serve

This is a particularly good fish cake recipe, great for using up leftovers, but I rarely make the same fish cakes twice. I use whatever fish I can get and vary the other ingredients, too. Sometimes I like to add chiles, or use different cooked vegetables, or different herbs. In summer we love to eat these outside with a tomato and basil salad and some flavored mayonnaise (see the flavored mayonnaise that accompanies the Dublin Bay Prawns on page 16). In winter I prefer them with an herb butter melting over the top.

Scrub the potatoes, but do not peel them. Place in a large saucepan, cover with cold water, and add a good pinch of salt. Bring the water to a boil and cook the potatoes for 10 minutes. Then pour out all but about 1 inch (3cm) of the water and continue to cook the potatoes over very low heat. Don't be tempted to stick a knife into them at any stage to see if they are cooked—the skins will split and the potatoes will just break up and become soggy if you do. About 20 minutes later, when you think the potatoes might be cooked, test them with a skewer; if they are soft, take them off the heat and drain them.

Peel the potatoes while they are still hot, holding them in a clean kitchen towel to avoid scalding your hands. Mash them immediately and transfer to a large bowl.

Meanwhile, place the fish in a wide, shallow saucepan and add 6 tablespoons of the butter, the wine, and the lemon juice. Season with salt and pepper, then cover with a lid and gently poach over low heat for 10 to 15 minutes, until the fish is cooked through. Carefully remove the fish from the pan and set aside to cool a little. Turn up the heat to high and boil the poaching liquid until it has reduced by half.

In the meantime, melt 2 tablespoons of the remaining butter in a small frying pan over medium heat. Add the mushrooms and sauté for 8 to 10 minutes, until soft and golden, seasoning with salt and pepper. Set aside and allow to cool a little.

Add the fish, reduced poaching liquid, and cooked mushrooms to the mashed potatoes along with the shrimp, egg yolks, mustard, and herbs. Gently mix everything together, breaking the fish up as you go but being careful not to mash it up too much. Season to taste with salt and pepper.

recipe continues overleaf

Shape the mixture into eight patties, each about 3 inches (8cm) wide and ¾ inch (2cm) thick, and arrange on a baking sheet or large plate. Cover with plastic wrap (cling film) and place in the fridge for about 1 hour to firm up. (The fish cakes can be prepared up to this stage in advance and either frozen or kept in the fridge for up to 24 hours.)

Combine the olive oil and remaining 2 tablespoons butter in a large, nonstick frying pan over medium-low heat and very gently fry the fish cakes for about 5 minutes on each side, or until golden and warmed through, adding a little more oil or butter to the pan during cooking if necessary.

Divide the fish cakes among the serving plates, add some salad greens to each plate, and serve immediately with lemon wedges and flavored mayonnaise (page 16) or Herb Butters (below).

Herb butters

Vegetarian

Each recipe **Makes** about 6 tablespoons (85g)

Preparation time: 5 minutes

FOR THE DILL BUTTER

5 tablespoons (75g) butter, softened

1 heaping tablespoon finely chopped fresh dill

Squeeze of lemon juice

Salt and freshly ground black pepper

FOR THE GARLIC AND HERB BUTTER

5 tablespoons (75g) butter, softened

3 cloves garlic, crushed

1 heaping tablespoon finely chopped mixed fresh herbs

Salt and freshly ground black pepper

Herb butter is easy to make, using whatever herbs are on hand. To store, spoon it onto some waxed paper, roll into a sausage shape, securing the ends, and pop in the fridge or freezer. Slice the butter as you need it.

Dill butter

Mash the butter with a fork in a small bowl to soften. Stir in the dill, along with a good squeeze of lemon juice and a little salt and pepper. Store in the fridge or freezer until ready to use.

Garlic and herb butter

Mash the butter with a fork in a small bowl to soften. Stir in the garlic, herbs, and a little salt and pepper. Store in the fridge or freezer until ready to use.

Fish stew

Serves 4 to 6

Preparation time: 15 minutes

Cooking time: 20 minutes

1 pound (450g) mussels

4 large tomatoes

4 tablespoons olive oil

7 ounces (200g) leeks, trimmed and cut into ⅜-inch (7mm) thick slices

1 red bell pepper, seeded and cut into ½- to ¾-inch (1–2cm) dice

Salt and freshly ground black pepper

1¼ cups (300ml) chicken stock (page 35) or fish stock

Good pinch of granulated or superfine (caster) sugar

12 raw, peeled jumbo shrimp, langoustines, or tiger prawns (about 8 ounces/225g in total)

11 ounces (300g) skinless white fish fillets, such as cod or haddock, cut into ¾-inch (2cm) chunks

2 tablespoons chopped parsley, to serve

This is a lovely light fish stew that just cries out for crusty bread to mop up all the delicious juices. Use whatever seafood is at its freshest—a combination of contrasting tastes and textures is what you're aiming for. Serve with Brown Soda Bread (page 227) or Ballymaloe Brown Yeast Bread (page 230).

First prepare the mussels. Rinse the shells in cold running water a couple of times to wash away any sand or grit. Give them a scrub to dislodge any barnacles or bits of weed, then remove the "beard" with a tug or a sharp knife. Discard any that are open and won't close when tapped against a hard surface.

Peel the tomatoes by scoring a cross at the top of each tomato with a sharp knife, then placing in a bowl and covering with boiling water. Leave in the water for 15 to 20 seconds, then drain, rinse in cold water, and peel the skin from each tomato. Chop the peeled tomatoes into small pieces and set aside.

Pour the olive oil into a large saucepan on medium heat, add the leeks and red pepper and season with salt and pepper. Cook for 4 minutes or until a little softened, then add the chopped tomatoes, stock, and sugar. Bring to a boil, then reduce the heat, cover with a lid, and cook for 7 to 8 minutes more or until the tomatoes are soft.

Tip in the mussels, shrimp, and fish, bring back up to a boil, then reduce the heat, cover with the lid, and simmer gently for 2 to 3 minutes or until the fish and seafood are cooked. (The fish and shrimp should be opaque and the mussels opened—discard any that remain closed.)

Season to taste, sprinkle over the parsley and serve with chunks of crusty bread.

Fish pie

Serves 4 to 6

Preparation time: 15 minutes

Cooking time: 1 hour 10 minutes

1 large onion, peeled and chopped

1¾ pounds (800g) skinless fish fillets, either one type or a mixture, such as salmon, cod, whiting, hake, or haddock

⅔ cup (150ml) white wine

Juice of ½ lemon

9 tablespoons (125g) butter, diced

Salt and freshly ground black pepper

5 ounces (150g) mushrooms, sliced

1 cup (225ml) heavy or whipping (double or regular) cream

1 heaping tablespoon Dijon mustard

4 tablespoons finely chopped mixed herbs, such as chives, parsley, tarragon, thyme, or dill

Creamy Mashed Potato (page 166)

This is the fish pie that my husband Isaac makes, and it's a wonderful family supper. The rich creamy fish filling is offset by the lemon juice and Dijon mustard. This fish pie can be made in advance, not cooked, and kept in the freezer for up to three months.

Preheat the oven to 350°F (180°C/Gas mark 4).

Put the onion in the bottom of a large saucepan and lay the fish on top in an even layer (cutting to fit, if necessary). Pour in the wine, add the lemon juice (the liquid is unlikely to cover the fish, but that's fine), scatter three-quarters of the butter over the top, and season with salt and pepper. Cover with a lid and simmer over low heat for 15 to 20 minutes, until the fish is cooked.

In the meantime, melt the remaining butter in a small frying pan over low heat and sauté the mushrooms for 5 to 6 minutes, until softened. Season well with salt and pepper.

Using a slotted spoon, carefully transfer the fish from the saucepan (leaving the onions and cooking liquid in the pan) to an 8-inch (22cm) square ovenproof dish or divide among four to six individual gratin dishes. While there is no need to flake the fish, you needn't worry if the fish breaks up as you move it.

Add the cream to the onions and cooking liquid in the pan and continue to simmer, with the lid off, for 10 to 15 minutes, until the sauce is reduced and thick enough to coat the back of a spoon. Stir in the mustard, herbs, and sautéed mushrooms and check the seasoning.

Pour the sauce over the fish in the dish (or dishes) and then spoon over the mashed potato, spreading with the back of a spoon or fork. Alternatively, pipe the mashed potatoes over the fish with a pastry bag and tip for a more professional-looking finish. (The fish pie can be prepared to this stage, left to cool, and then placed in the fridge overnight until you are ready to bake, if wished.)

Bake in the oven for about 30 minutes, or until bubbling and golden on top. Add about 10 minutes if the pie has been chilled. Serve immediately.

Chicken casserole with cheesy herb dumplings

Serves 6 to 8

Preparation time: 30 minutes

Cooking time: 1 hour 10 minutes

1 whole chicken (4 pounds/1.8kg)

Salt and freshly ground black pepper

2 tablespoons olive oil

12 ounces (350g) thick-cut or unsliced bacon, cut into ½- to ¾-inch (1–2cm) chunks

1 large onion, coarsely chopped

2 large carrots, sliced ¾-inch (2cm) thick on the diagonal

3 cups (700ml) chicken stock (page 35) or vegetable stock (page 34)

Few sprigs of thyme

FOR THE CHEESY HERB DUMPLINGS

2¾ cups (350g) all-purpose (plain) flour, plus extra for dusting

1 teaspoon baking soda (bicarbonate of soda)

1 teaspoon salt

2 tablespoons finely chopped mixed fresh herbs, such as parsley, thyme, rosemary, tarragon, or chives

1¼ cups (300ml) buttermilk or soured milk (see tip on page 228)

4 tablespoons finely grated cheddar cheese

This is such a perfect family meal: a steaming pot for the center of the table, just the kind of food I want on a blustery day. It's really easy to make and the dumplings are a fantastic alternative to potatoes or bread. I like to serve this dish with a green salad.

Preheat the oven to 350°F (180°C/Gas mark 4).

Remove the breasts from the chicken and cut them in half. Remove the leg portions and divide them into thighs and drumsticks. This will make eight chicken pieces in total. Season them well with salt and pepper.

Pour the olive oil into a large Dutch oven or flameproof casserole over high heat, add the bacon, and fry for 1 to 2 minutes, until crisp. Remove with a slotted spoon and drain on paper towels. Add the chicken in batches and sear on each side until golden, then remove. Add the onion and carrots and fry for 2 to 3 minutes, until golden.

Return the bacon and chicken to the Dutch oven, pour in the stock, add the thyme, and season with salt and pepper. Bring slowly to a boil, cover with a tight-fitting lid, and bake in the oven for 20 minutes.

In the meantime, prepare the dumplings. Sift the flour, baking soda, and salt into a large bowl and stir in the herbs. Make a well in the center and pour in most of the buttermilk (leaving about ¼ cup/50ml) in the measuring cup). Using one hand with your fingers outstretched like a claw, bring the flour and liquid together, adding a little more buttermilk, if necessary. Don't knead the mixture or it will become too heavy. The dough should be soft but not too wet and sticky.

Tip the dough onto a floured work surface and bring together, forming it into a round. Using a rolling pin, roll the dough out to a thickness of about ¾ inch (2cm). With a 2-inch (5cm) cookie cutter, stamp out 10 to 12 dumplings, or divide the dough into 10 to 12 pieces and roll each one between your hands into a small ball.

Remove the Dutch oven from the oven and turn the heat up to 450°F (230°C/Gas mark 8). Arrange the dumplings on top, leaving slight gaps to allow for spreading. Sprinkle with the cheese. Return to the oven, uncovered, for 10 minutes. Decrease the heat to 400°F (200°C/Gas mark 6) and bake for another 20 minutes, or until the dumplings are crisp and golden and the chicken is cooked through.

Turkey and ham potato pie

Serves 6 to 8

Preparation time: 10 minutes

Cooking time: 1 hour

4 tablespoons (50g) butter

1 onion, finely chopped

1 pound (450g) mushrooms, sliced

1½ cups (350ml) heavy (double) cream

½ cup (100ml) turkey or chicken stock (page 35)

5 cups (1½ pounds/675g) mixed leftover cooked turkey and ham, cut into ½-inch (1cm) chunks

1 tablespoon chopped fresh tarragon or marjoram

Salt and freshly ground black pepper

Creamy Mashed Potato (page 166)

This is a pie we tend to make after Christmas Day, when we have both leftover turkey and ham. We also call it St. Stephen's Day (the day after Christmas) Pie, and it's always incredibly popular in our house, even with the disappointment of Christmas being over! You can use chicken or another bird if you don't have leftover turkey. Try serving with Buttered Leeks (page 147) or Creamed Kale (page 147).

Preheat the oven to 350°F (180°C/Gas mark 4).

Melt 2 tablespoons of the butter in a large saucepan over low heat. Add the onion and fry gently for 8 to 10 minutes, until completely soft but not browned. Remove from the pan and set aside. Increase the heat and add the remaining 2 tablespoons butter to the pan. Tip the mushrooms into the pan and sauté for 4 to 5 minutes, until they are soft and golden brown (you may need to do this in two batches).

Return the onion to the pan and pour in the cream and stock. Bring to a boil, then decrease the heat, and simmer for 3 to 4 minutes, until the sauce has thickened a little. Add the turkey, ham, and tarragon and season to taste with salt and pepper. Pour into a shallow 3-quart (3l) gratin dish set on a baking sheet and spread evenly. Top with the mashed potato, spooning it on in dollops and spreading with a fork.

Bake for 25 to 30 minutes in the oven, until golden brown on top and bubbling hot.

Rachel's tip

Rather than making one large pie, divide the ingredients among six to eight individual pie dishes. This is also particularly handy if you choose to freeze them (fully made with the mashed potato on top). Then you can take them out as you need them.

Homemade pork sausages with colcannon and applesauce

Serves 4 (makes about 12 sausages)

Preparation time: 15 minutes

Cooking time: 40 minutes

1 pound (450g) fatty ground (minced) pork

1 cup (50g) fresh bread crumbs

1 egg, lightly beaten

1 clove garlic, crushed

1 tablespoon chopped fresh parsley or marjoram

Salt and freshly ground black pepper

3 tablespoons olive oil or sunflower oil

FOR THE COLCANNON

3 pounds (1.5kg) baking or russet (floury) potatoes, scrubbed

½ cup (100g) butter

1 pound, 2 ounces (500g) green cabbage, outer leaves removed

2 tablespoons water

1 cup (250ml) milk, heated

2 tablespoons chopped fresh parsley

Salt and freshly ground black pepper

FOR THE APPLESAUCE

1 large cooking apple (12 ounces /350g), peeled, cored, and coarsely chopped

1 tablespoon water

2 to 4 tablespoons (25–50g) sugar

For me there is nothing quite so comforting as bangers and mash, and these homemade sausages are ever so tasty and easy to make. Colcannon, which is a traditional Halloween-time Irish dish of mashed potato with cabbage, is perfect winter food.

To make the sausages, mix together the pork, bread crumbs, egg, garlic, and parsley. Season with salt and pepper. Fry a tiny bit of the mixture in a pan with a little olive or sunflower oil to see if the seasoning is good.

Divide the mixture into twelve portions and shape each one into a sausage. Place on a baking sheet or plate and set aside until you want to cook them. (Chilling them for a day in the fridge is fine, or you can freeze them.)

To make the colcannon, cook the potatoes, covered, in boiling salted water for 10 minutes. Then drain three-quarters of the water and continue to cook over low heat with the lid on for another 20 to 30 minutes until cooked. Test using a skewer or feel with your fingers; avoid stabbing the potatoes with a knife because this will make them break up. When cooked, drain all the remaining water, peel, and mash with ¼ cup of the butter while hot. I usually hold the potato on a fork and peel with a knife if they are hot.

Meanwhile, cook the cabbage. Cut the cabbage into quarters, then cut out the core. Thinly slice the cabbage across the grain. Heat a saucepan, add the remaining ¼ cup butter, water, and the sliced cabbage. Toss over medium heat for 5 to 7 minutes, until just cooked. Add to the potatoes, then add most of the hot milk and the parsley, keeping some of the milk back in case you do not need it all.

Season to taste and beat until creamy and smooth, adding more milk if necessary.

While the potatoes are cooking, make the applesauce and cook the sausages. To make the applesauce, put the apple in a small saucepan with the water. Cover and cook over gentle heat (stir every now and then) until the apple has broken down to a mush. Add sugar to taste.

To cook the sausages, heat a frying pan on a low to medium heat, add 2 tablespoons of the olive oil, and gently fry the sausages for 12 to 15 minutes, until golden on all sides and cooked on the inside. Serve with the colcannon and applesauce.

Dublin coddle

Serves 4 to 6

Preparation time: 5 minutes

Cooking time: 30 minutes

12 ounces (350g) potato, peeled and cut into ¾-inch (2cm) cubes (more or less)

1¼ cups (200g) finely chopped onion

8 ounces (225g) breakfast sausages, each cut into 4 pieces

2½ cups (600ml) leftover bacon cooking liquid, chicken stock (page 35), or water

Salt and freshly ground black pepper

3½ ounces (100g) leftover boiled or fried bacon, torn or cut into ½- to ¾-inch (1–2cm) chunks (more or less)

1 tablespoon finely chopped fresh parsley

Coddle is a simple Irish dish long associated with Dublin and spoken of in rapturous tones by many of us from the city. It is a mixture of potato, bacon, onion, and sausage all cooked in a flavorful broth. This is a recipe from my husband Isaac, which he made one Monday using leftover bacon and the cooking water from the previous evening's boiled bacon (see page 112). The use of the cooking water gives this coddle recipe real depth of flavor, but it's incredibly simple to put together. If you don't have leftover boiled bacon, you can make this dish using fried slices (rashers) or cubes (lardoons) of bacon and chicken stock or, even, water.

Put the potato, onion, and sausages in a large saucepan and add the bacon cooking water. Add a little salt and pepper (but not too much if you're using bacon cooking water). Place over medium heat and bring to a boil, then simmer for about 30 minutes, until the potatoes are just tender. Add the cooked bacon and cook for another few minutes. Stir in the parsley, season to taste, and serve immediately.

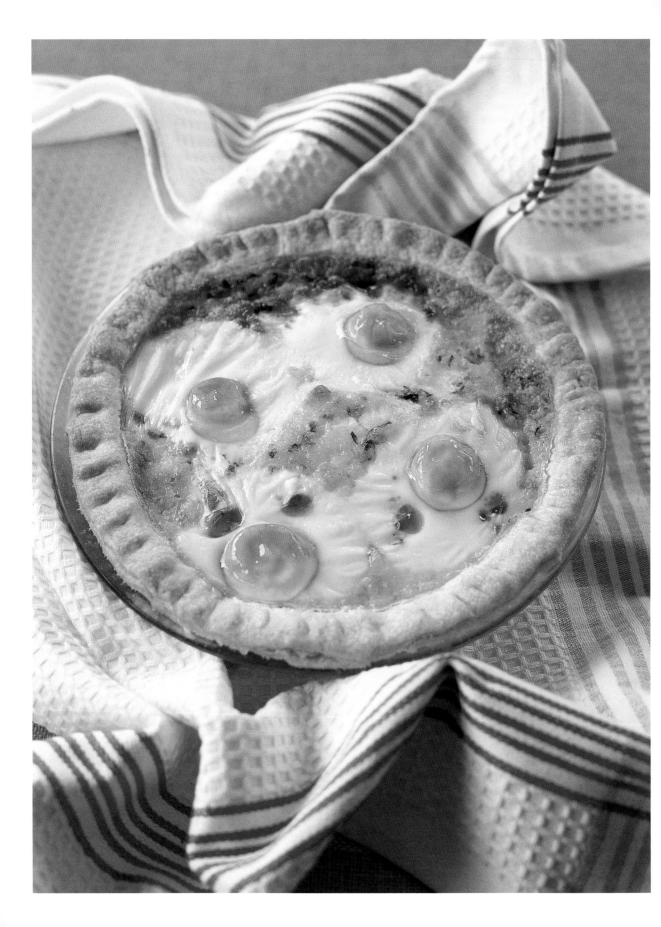

Ham and egg pie

Serves 6 to 8

Preparation time: 20 minutes

Cooking time: 40 minutes

Shortcrust Pastry, (page 72)

1 tablespoon (15g) butter

1 onion, chopped

6 eggs

⅓ cup (75ml) heavy (double) cream

5 ounces (150g) cooked ham or bacon, sliced into ½ by ¾-inch (1 by 2cm) pieces

1 tablespoon chopped fresh parsley

Salt and freshly ground black pepper

This is a lovely, old-fashioned picnic pie. You can serve it for lunch, but it travels well for a picnic. This is the sort of thing people used to make to bring to work with them; in fact, you could do the same! If you have any left over, it makes a handsome breakfast. Try serving with Tomato Relish (page 20) and a green salad.

Preheat the oven to 350°F (180°C/Gas mark 4).

Roll out the pastry and line a 10-inch (25cm) pie pan. Trim the pastry so that it is a bit bigger than the pan, then fold up the edges slightly so that you have a slight lip all the way around. This will prevent the cream from running out when you put the pie in the oven. Refrigerate while you prepare the filling.

For the filling, melt the butter in a small saucepan over low heat, add the onions, and cook until soft, 5 to 8 minutes. Whisk two of the eggs in a bowl, add the cream, the cooked onions, chopped ham, and parsley. Season with salt and pepper. Pour this into the pastry. Carefully break the remaining eggs onto the tart, trying to keep the egg yolks intact.

Bake for 25 to 35 minutes, until the custard is set in the center and the eggs on top are just cooked. Serve warm or allow to cool and pack for a picnic. Cut slices of the tart straight from the pan.

Savory shortcrust pastry

Vegetarian

Makes 1 pound (450g)

Preparation time: 55 minutes
(including cooling)

Cooking time: 17 to 22 minutes

2 cups (250g) all-purpose (plain)
flour

9 tablespoons (125g) butter, diced
and softened

½ to 1 egg, beaten

This makes enough to line one (11-inch/28cm) square or one (10-inch /25cm) round pan (with a little left over), or two (8-inch/20cm) square pans (it is best if they have removable bases). Uncooked pastry freezes perfectly, so it is handy to have some in the freezer. It will also keep in the fridge for a couple of days.

Combine the flour and butter in a food processor. Whiz for a few seconds, then add half the beaten egg and continue whizzing. You might need to add a little more egg, but don't add too much—the pastry should just come together. (If making by hand, rub the butter into the flour, then use your hands to bring it together with the egg.) Flatten out the ball of dough to a thickness of about 1¼ inches (3cm), wrap or cover with plastic wrap (cling film), and refrigerate for at least 30 minutes.

When you are ready to roll the pastry, remove from the fridge. Place the pastry between two sheets of plastic wrap, which should be bigger than your tart pan. Using a rolling pin, roll it out until it is no thicker than ⅛ inch (3mm). Make sure to keep it round, if the pan is round, and large enough to line the bottom and sides of the pan.

Remove the top layer of plastic wrap and place the pastry upside-down (plastic wrap side facing up) in the tart pan. Press into the edges, plastic wrap still attached and, using your thumbnail, cut the pastry on the edge of the pan to give a neat finish. Remove the plastic wrap and pop the pastry in the freezer for at least 10 minutes.

Blind baking
Blind baking is a way of partially cooking a pastry shell before adding its filling. Preheat the oven to 350°F(180°C/Gas mark 4). Line the pastry with waxed paper when cold (leaving plenty to come up the sides), fill with pie weights or dried beans (you can use these over and over), and bake for 15 to 20 minutes, until the pastry feels dry. Remove the paper and beans, brush with a little leftover beaten egg, and return to the oven for 2 minutes. Take out of the oven and put to one side while you prepare the filling. This can be made a day in advance.

Variation
Sweet pastry: Use the recipe for savory pastry, but add 3 tablespoons plus 1 teaspoon (25g) confectioners' (icing) sugar to the flour and butter in the food processor at the start of the recipe.

Pork chops with sage and apple

Serves 4

Preparation time: 10 minutes

Cooking time: 15 minutes

2 tablespoons (25g) butter

2 tablespoons extra virgin olive oil

4 pork loin chops (each about ⅝ inch/1.5cm thick)

Salt and freshly ground black pepper

2 apples, peeled and cut into ¼-inch (5mm) slices

¾ cup (200ml) hard cider

4 tablespoons crème fraîche or sour cream

4 teaspoons chopped fresh sage

Sage and apple are the autumnal flavors of Ireland. Sweet apples are the perfect partner for pork. Smooth applesauce, of course, goes well with roast pork, but here there are apple slices, which retain their bite. I think it's especially fitting that this recipe then uses cider to finish everything off. If you can, use our delicious dry Irish cider. You could serve this with Sautéed Potatoes with Caramelized Onions (page 162), Roast Garlic Colcannon (page 170), Root Vegetable Mash (page 165), or Buttered Cabbage (page 144).

Combine the butter and olive oil in a large frying pan over high heat. When the butter starts to foam, place the chops in the pan and season with salt and pepper. Cook on one side for 2 to 3 minutes, until golden underneath, then turn over and season again.

Add the apple slices to the pan, nestling them in among the pork. Cook for about 5 minutes, tossing the slices regularly, until the apples are golden and softened and the chops are cooked through.

Pour in the cider and stir in the crème fraîche and sage. Bring to a simmer and allow to bubble for a couple of minutes, or until slightly thickened. Season with salt and pepper to taste and serve.

Pork and mushroom pie with gentle spices

Serves 4

Preparation time: 15 minutes

Cooking time: 1¾ hours

2 tablespoons (25g) butter

2 onions, chopped

Salt and freshly ground pepper

1 teaspoon ground cumin

1 teaspoon ground coriander

1½ pounds (680g) pork (shoulder or leg, fat removed), cut into ½- to ¾-inch (1–2cm) cubes

1 cup (250ml) chicken stock (page 35)

1 tablespoon extra virgin olive oil

11 ounces (300g) button mushrooms, sliced, left whole, or quartered

1 cup (250ml) light (single) cream

1 tablespoon chopped fresh parsley

FOR THE ROUX

2 tablespoons (25g) butter

3 tablespoons (20g) all-purpose (plain) flour

FOR THE TOPPING

11 ounces (300g) puff or shortcrust pie (flaky) pastry, rolled ¼ inch (5mm) thick

1 egg, beaten

OR

Creamy Mashed Potato (page 166)

Cumin and coriander seem to be the two spices I reach for the most and run out of most often, they both go well with pork. The filling for the pie can be made a day in advance and left in the fridge, giving the spices time to infuse the meat. Then cover with mashed potato or buttery pastry.

Preheat the oven to 325°F (160°C/Gas mark 3).

To make the filling, melt the butter in a medium-size Dutch oven or flameproof casserole dish, add the onions, and season with salt and pepper. Cover and sweat over low heat for 5 minutes. Turn up the heat and add the cumin, coriander, and pork. Toss for a few minutes until the pork changes color, then add the stock. Cover and bake in the oven for 45 to 60 minutes, until the pork is tender.

While the pork is cooking, heat the olive oil in a pan over high heat and toss in the mushrooms. Cook for a few minutes until they are pale golden. Add to the pork after it has baked for 30 minutes.

When the pork is tender, remove the pork and mushrooms from their cooking liquid and set aside in a dish in a warm place. Add the cream to the juices in the pan and boil with the lid off for a few minutes until the flavor intensifies.

To thicken the sauce, first make the roux. Melt the butter in a medium-size saucepan over medium heat. Add the flour, stirring, and allow it to cook for 2 minutes then remove from the heat. Slowly stir the roux into the boiling cooking liquid. Add the chopped parsley and return the pork and mushrooms. Season to taste and spoon into individual gratin dishes or a large pie dish.

For a pastry topping, preheat the oven to 450°F (230°C/Gas mark 8). For a mashed potato topping, preheat it to 350°F (180°C/Gas mark 4).

For a pastry top, cut the pastry to the same size as the top of the pie dish and arrange over the filling. Make a hole in the center for steam to escape. Brush with the beaten egg to glaze. Bake for 10 minutes, then turn down the oven temperature to 375°F (190°C/Gas mark 5) and bake for about 20 minutes, until the pastry is golden brown.

For a mashed potato top, arrange the mashed potato on top of the filling and lightly score the surface. Bake for 30 to 40 minutes, until golden brown on top and bubbling hot.

Lamb chops with parsley and mint sauce

Serves 4 to 6

Preparation time: 5 minutes

Cooking time: 10 minutes

8 to 12 lamb loin chops

4 tablespoons extra virgin olive oil

Salt and freshly ground black
 pepper

FOR THE PARSLEY AND MINT SAUCE

Handful of mint leaves

2 handfuls of parsley leaves

2 tablespoons capers, drained and
 rinsed

8 canned anchovies

6 tablespoons extra virgin olive oil

2 to 4 tablespoons freshly squeezed
 lemon juice

Salt and freshly ground black
 pepper

A parsley and mint sauce is an easy way of adding flavor to lamb chops. The anchovies give the sauce a wonderful depth that works particularly well with lamb and doesn't taste at all fishy. The mint and parsley bring freshness while the capers give the sauce their own particular punchy flavor. You can make the sauce ahead and it will keep in a jar for up to two weeks in the fridge. Do take it out of the fridge about half an hour or so before serving, to give the flavors a chance to wake up.

The sauce would also be an excellent accompaniment to grilled steak, roast chicken, or pan-fried mackerel. You could also serve with Pea and Scallion Champ (page 169).

To make the sauce, combine the herbs, capers, anchovies, olive oil, and 2 tablespoons of the lemon juice in a food processor. Whiz for a minute, then add salt and pepper or more lemon juice to taste. If you don't have a food processor you can chop everything finely by hand and mix together.

Place a frying pan or griddle pan over high heat. While it is heating, drizzle the lamb chops with the olive oil and season with salt and pepper. Place in the hot pan and cook for 2 to 4 minutes on each side, until just pink in the center. Serve immediately with a drizzling of the sauce.

Irish stew

Serves 4 to 6

Preparation time: 10 minutes

Cooking time: 1½ to 2 hours

3⅓ pounds (1.5kg) mutton or lamb chops from the neck or shoulder, still on the bone, cut about ¾ inch (1.5cm) thick

3 tablespoons extra virgin olive oil

3 carrots, cut into thick slices at an angle, or 12 small baby carrots, scrubbed and left whole

12 baby onions, or 3 to 4 medium onions, cut into quarters through the root, which should keep the wedges intact

Salt and freshly ground black pepper

1⅔ cups (400ml) lamb stock, chicken stock (page 35), or water

8 to 12 potatoes, peeled, and halved if very large

Sprig of thyme

1 tablespoon chopped fresh parsley

1 tablespoon snipped fresh chives

The definitive recipe for Irish stew simply doesn't exist because each household has its own family recipe. It is said, however, that people in the south of Ireland always add carrots, but people north of County Tipperary do not. Many people make their stew by placing alternate layers of meat, onions, carrots, and potatoes, seasoned with salt and pepper, in a pot, covering with water, and stewing gently for a couple of hours. If you sear the meat and vegetables before stewing, as we do at Ballymaloe, it seals in the delicious sweet flavors.

Preheat the oven to 325°F (160°C/Gas mark 3).

Cut the chops in half, but keep the bones intact as they will give great flavor. Heat the olive oil in a medium to large Dutch oven or flameproof casserole. Toss in the meat and cook for a minute on both sides, until nice and brown. Remove the meat and set aside. Add the carrots and onions to the hot oil and cook for a couple of minutes, seasoning with salt and pepper. Return the meat to the pot. Add the stock and bring to a boil. Put the potatoes in, season again with salt and pepper, and place a sprig of thyme on top.

Cover and bake in the oven for 1½ to 2 hours, until the meat is very tender. When it is cooked, pour off the cooking liquid and allow it to sit for a minute until the fat floats to the top; adding a cube of ice will help speed this up. Spoon off the fat and pour the juices back over the stew. Add the chopped herbs and serve.

Rachel's tip
If the potatoes are quite small, add them 20 to 30 minutes after the stew starts cooking to avoid them breaking up.

Special family dinners

For me there are few things more gratifying than cooking a special dinner for my whole family. Often it's a particular family member's favorite, such as Isaac's Hot Buttered Lobster (page 90), the Pot-roasted Duck Legs (page 106) that my son Joshua loves so much, or a roast chicken (page 96) that the whole family adores. Making fabulous meals should never be reserved just for serving guests. Your family is just as deserving, if not more deserving, of such treats!

These are great recipes but they're never fussy. They're big, warming, convivial dishes that are perfect for sharing. There are some real Irish classics in here. Boiled Bacon and Cabbage (page 112) is a traditional dish that is still hugely popular, and Beef and Red Wine Hot Pot (page 130) is a hearty supper beloved of everyone whose mother made it for them.

You'll also find lots of fantastic fish recipes in this chapter. Being an island, Ireland offers a wonderful selection of fresh fish wherever you live in the country. I think the best way of serving such great fish is to not do too much with it and serve it quite simply, with perhaps an Herb Butter (page 56), or Hollandaise Sauce (page 12).

Salmon with capers and dill

Serves 4

Preparation time: 5 minutes

Cooking time: 10 minutes

4 tablespoons (50g) butter, diced

4 (4-ounce/125g) salmon fillets (with the skin left on, if you wish)

Salt and freshly ground black pepper

4 tablespoons capers, drained and rinsed

2 tablespoons freshly squeezed lemon juice mixed with 6 to 8 tablespoons water

4 teaspoons chopped fresh dill

I always have a jar of capers in my fridge—they're a great shortcut to a good punchy flavor. Here, they cut through the rich oily fish. This dish can be made in just a few minutes, and I like to serve it simply with some boiled new potatoes. Instead of salmon, it would be just as good with fresh mackerel, an equally oily fish. The fish goes particularly well with Pea and Scallion Champ (page 169).

Place a frying pan over medium-high heat. When it is hot, add a couple of pats (knobs) of butter, very quickly followed by the salmon, skin side down. Fry for 3 to 4 minutes, until golden brown underneath. Turn over, season with salt and pepper, and fry for another couple of minutes, or until the fish is just cooked through. (The timing will depend on the thickness of the salmon fillets and heat of the pan.)

Add the capers, along with the remaining butter, and lemon juice mixture and boil for 1 minute. Season to taste, adding more lemon juice or water, if necessary. Transfer the salmon onto warmed plates, stir the chopped dill into the sauce, and pour over the fish to serve.

Pan-fried mackerel with herb butter

Serves 4

Preparation time: 5 minutes

Cooking time: 5 minutes

8 mackerel fillets, with the skins on

⅔ cup (75g) all-purpose (plain) flour, seasoned with salt and pepper

2 tablespoons (25g) butter, softened

Lemon wedges, to serve

FOR THE HERB BUTTER

½ cup (100g) butter, softened

2 tablespoons chopped fresh herbs

1 tablespoon freshly squeezed lemon juice

My son Joshua will often fish for mackerel off the pier in late summer when the mackerel are at their best. He and his friends will bring back a few delicious fish, which he loves to cook himself. It is said the sun should never set on a mackerel; certainly it is a fish that must be eaten as fresh as possible. This is a simple but absolutely divine way to serve one of my favorite fish. Serve with Creamy Mashed Potato (page 166) and a green salad or Pea Purée (page 150) if you'd desire.

To make the herb butter, cream the butter in a bowl and add the chopped herbs and the lemon juice. Roll into a sausage shape and wrap in waxed paper (greaseproof paper) or plastic wrap (cling film). Put into the freezer to chill quickly.

Place a frying pan or a grill-pan over high heat and wait for it to get very hot. When the pan is hot, dip the fillets in the seasoned flour and shake off the excess. Spread the flesh side (not the skin side) with a little soft butter and place butter-side down on the hot pan. Cook for a couple of minutes, until crisp and golden, then turn over and cook the other side for another 2 to 3 minutes, turning down the heat if the pan is getting too hot.

Serve on hot plates with one or two slices of herb butter slowly melting on the fish, with a wedge of lemon on the side.

Trout baked in parchment paper

Serves 4

Preparation time: 5 minutes

Cooking time: 15 minutes

3½ tablespoons (40g) butter, softened

2 tablespoons chopped fresh parsley

1 tablespoon chopped fresh thyme

1 tablespoon chopped fresh dill

Salt and freshly ground black pepper

4 trout fillets (or salmon or mullet), about 4 ounces (125g) each

Trout in all their different colors have always been eaten in Ireland. There are lakes and rivers all over the country full of this delicious and delicately flavored fish. Trout is available in fishmongers or, of course, you can catch it yourself!

By cooking fish in a parcel of baking parchment, all the flavors from the fish and this herb butter are sealed in. It also ensures the fish is kept perfectly moist. I love serving this dish to guests and watching each person open their own parcel and breathe in the gorgeous aromas from the herbs and fish.

Try serving with Creamy Mashed Potato (page 166) and Minted Fava Beans (page 150) or Pea Purée (page 150).

Preheat the oven to 425°F (220°C/Gas mark 7).

For each serving, cut out a piece of parchment paper or aluminum foil measuring about 12 inches (30cm) square.

To make the herb butter, mix together the butter, parsley, thyme, and dill in a bowl and season with salt and pepper.

Place a piece of fish in the center of the paper and add a spoonful (a quarter) of the herb butter. Fold the square in half to enclose the filling and then fold in the edges to seal and form a parcel. The finished parcel should be semicircular in shape, looking rather like a Cornish pasty. Repeat for the other pieces of fish and place on a baking sheet.

Bake for 12 to 14 minutes, until the fish is just opaque all the way through. You'll need to open one to check; this can be yours. Place the parcels on serving plates for people to open for themselves.

Rachel's tip

You could also make this dish with whole trout, though they will take longer to cook, about 25 to 30 minutes.

Hot buttered lobster

Serves 4

Preparation time: 30 minutes

Cooking time: 30 minutes

2 (2-pound/900g) live lobsters

Salt and freshly ground black pepper

1 carrot, sliced

1 onion, sliced

2 celery stalks, sliced

2½ cups (600ml) water

2½ cups (600ml) dry white wine

2 sprigs of parsley

2 sprigs of thyme

1 bay leaf

A few peppercorns

4 tablespoons (50g) butter

Juice of 1 lemon, plus wedges to garnish

I think this is the best way of serving lobster—it's simply about presenting that wonderfully sweet meat of the most impressive of shellfish. I adore lobster straight from the sea. This decadent dish is strictly for special occasions. It's important that when you're cooking the steamed lobster in the butter you allow the butter to get quite golden as that really intensifies the sweet flavor. Serve with nothing more than boiled new potatoes.

A couple of hours before you are ready to cook, put the lobsters in a plastic bag in the freezer. When it is time to cook them, bring a large saucepan of salted water (3 tablespoons salt to every 10 cups/2l water) to a boil.

Plunge the frozen lobsters directly into the boiling water and when they start to turn color from dark to browny orange, in about 10 minutes, remove them from the pan and discard the water.

Put the carrot, onion, celery, water, wine, herbs, and peppercorns into the same saucepan and bring to a boil. Add the lobsters and cover with the lid. Cook until they turn a very bright orange-red: For a 2-pound (900g) lobster, this will be about 20 minutes and for a 3-pound (1.3kg) lobster, this will be about 30 minutes. When they are cooked, take them out of the pot and let them cool. Strain the cooking liquid and use as fish stock (it will freeze).

Once the lobsters are cool enough to handle, turn the lobster over so the softer belly is facing upward. With a large, sharp knife cut them in half lengthwise from head to the tail as evenly as possible. Extract all the meat from the head and from the tail and claws. You will need to use either a wooden mallet or the flat edge of a chopping knife blade to crack open the claws. Chop the meat into ¾-inch (2cm) chunks.

Clean the lobster shells (keeping the head and tail intact, if possible, to serve the lobster in) and pop into a low oven along with your plates just to heat up.

Melt the butter in a frying pan over high heat. When it's hot and foaming, add the lobster meat and toss for about a minute. Season with lemon juice and pepper. Using a slotted spoon, divide the lobster among the half shells on warmed plates, then spoon the juices over the lobster meat. Serve immediately with wedges of lemon and see your guests melt in ecstasy!

Ulster

In the long history of Irish food, the humble spud is relatively new to the Irish plate. The early Irish didn't know this vegetable; a typical meal for them would have been bread and milk, perhaps flavored with salted meat, cabbage, onion, and seaweed. It is the potato, however, with which we are so closely identified. Traditional to northwest Ireland is a dish known as boxty, or "poor-house bread" (see the recipe on page 168). It dates back to early 19th-century prefamine times when the watery "lumper" potato was abundant. Potatoes at the bottom of the barrel, perhaps past their best, were used to make poor-house bread. The potato was grated and mashed, then drained in a cotton pillow case that was hung from the door. The yellowish liquid was collected in a bowl below and used as a source of starch for washing clothes. The drained potatoes were mixed with flour and a grain of salt, then cooked on a cast-iron griddle over an open fire. A slice of boxty topped with a fried egg makes for a warm, filling winter's breakfast.

Armagh is in Orchard County. For more than 3,000 years, apple trees have grown in these fertile, loam soils. The orchards are bound by tall hedgerows that act as windbreakers to protect the young apple crop. In autumn, Armagh apple growers keep a close eye on the size and sweetness of their Bramley apples; the skin must be solid green with a reddish flush, the flesh a white color with a hint of green. October's harvest is celebrated with a traditional apple festival, and local people enjoy eating these tangy, firm apples in a variety of dishes: Armagh Bramley apple pie and Bramley Apple Soup are served with a glass of Armagh cider.

The home of the potato in Ulster is Comber, where the land is sheltered by the Mourne Mountains and the Ards Peninsula and protected from the sharp frosts by Strangford Lough. This micro-climate warms the soil. Comber potatoes are ready to lift in May, and locals anticipate early summer with a flurry of excitement and joy as these unique potatoes are ready to eat. The nutty, distinctive flavor is best tasted when these potatoes are seasoned and served with a round of fresh Irish butter. Many believe that champ—a traditional dish of mashed potatoes blended with scallions, butter, salt, and pepper (see the recipe on page 169)—is only authentic when made with Comber potatoes. By European law, Comber spuds are so unique that, like Champagne, their status is protected.

The unpolluted waters off Donegal and the north coast are replete with wild seafoods. For generations, coastal communities have gleaned carrageenan moss, winged kelp, razor clams, dulse (dillisk), periwinkles, cockles, oysters, mussels, and more. Home-smoking was a strong tradition in Ireland as a way to deal with a glut of fresh fish caught in the sea. Fish were rubbed with sea salt and stored in a cold shed near the house. During the lean winter months the dried fish would be sliced and enjoyed with boiled potatoes, cabbage, and Irish butter.

A special prize is reserved for the one hundred and fifty fishing families who live in the five provinces that touch the shores of Ireland's biggest lake, Lough Neagh, because it is in these waters that Europe's largest commercial wild eel fishery is found. The fishermen's cooperative operates a strictly controlled fishery to ensure the prospects of future generations of eel fishermen. Public houses such as the oldest thatched pub in Northern Ireland, the Crosskeys Inn, serve this salty, fatty fish to local people as a way to celebrate the end of the eel fishing season in October.

Steamed mussels with cream and herbs

Serves 4

Preparation time: 10 minutes

Cooking time: 10 minutes

5½ pounds (2.5kg) mussels

⅔ cup (150ml) heavy or whipping (double or regular) cream

1 tablespoon chopped fresh parsley

1 tablespoon chopped fresh chives

2 teaspoons chopped fresh thyme leaves

2 teaspoons chopped fresh fennel (the herb, not the bulb)

Everyone in our family adores mussels, and this dish is a convivial social food, with a great big bowl of steaming mussels in the center of the table and crusty bread to share. The novelty of removing each mussel from its shell can be very enticing for young and old alike. In this recipe you can use a mixture of your favorite fresh herbs or whatever you have on hand. Tarragon, chervil, dill, and marjoram all work perfectly, in addition to the ones suggested here. There is no need to season this dish because the juices from the mussels will probably be salty enough. Serve with Brown Soda Bread (page 227) or Ballymaloe Brown Yeast Bread (page 230).

Scrub the mussels very well, discarding any that are open and don't close when tapped against a hard surface. Remove the beard—the little fibrous tuft—from each mussel.

Pour the cream into a large saucepan and bring slowly to a boil. Stir in the herbs and add the mussels. Decrease the heat to a simmer, cover with a lid, and continue to cook over medium heat for 5 to 8 minutes, until all the mussels are completely open. (Discard any that remain closed.)

Scoop the mussels out into one large or four individual serving bowls and ladle the creamy juices over. Place another bowl on the table for the empty shells, some finger bowls, and lots of napkins.

Roast chicken with stuffing and gravy

Serves 4 to 6

Preparation time: 5 minutes

Cooking time: 1½ to 1¾ hours

Traditional Herb Stuffing (or one of the variations) (page 161)

1 whole chicken (3⅓ to 5 pounds/ 1.5–2.25kg)

1 tablespoon (15g) butter, softened

Salt and freshly ground black pepper

Chicken Gravy (page 98) or Tarragon Cream Sauce (page 99)

I'm often asked what dish most brings me back to my childhood, and it is without a doubt roast chicken. In the winter we always stuff the bird. In fact in many homes in Ireland, there'll be an outcry if there's no stuffing. In the summer, though, I often forgo the stuffing for something a little lighter—just a few cloves of garlic and a lemon.

Of course, roast chicken is fantastic with a simple gravy, but why not experiment with a cream sauce, such as the Tarragon Cream Sauce on page 99—most definitely Isaac's favorite!

Serve with Granny's Roasted Herbed Potatoes (page 158), Sticky Cumin and Apricot Roast Carrots and Parsnips (page 155), Buttered Cabbage (page 144), and Root Vegetable Mash (page165).

First make the stuffing (if using). Allow to cool.

Preheat the oven to 350°F (180°C/Gas mark 4).

Spoon the cooled stuffing into the chicken cavity and place the chicken in a roasting pan. Smear the butter over the skin and sprinkle with salt and pepper. Roast for 1½ to 1¾ hours (allowing about 20 minutes per pound/450g), basting occasionally, until cooked through. If the skin begins to look quite dark during cooking, cover the chicken with some aluminum foil or parchment paper.

To check whether the chicken is fully cooked, stick a skewer into the thigh with a spoon placed underneath to catch the juices; the juices should run clear. Also, the legs should feel quite loose on the bird. When cooked, transfer the chicken to a serving plate and leave to rest, covered with foil and in the oven at the lowest temperature, if possible, while you make the gravy or sauce using the juices of the cooked chicken.

To serve, spoon the stuffing out of the chicken into a serving bowl or onto a plate. Carve the chicken and serve with the stuffing and gravy or any other accompanying sauce.

Rachel's tip
Always buy as good a chicken as you can afford, remembering not only that this is going to be great on the day you cook it, but also that you can then use the leftovers in a soup, pie, or pasta sauce, and even make a stock out of the carcass.

Chicken gravy

Makes about 1⅔ cups (400ml)

Preparation time: 5 minutes

Cooking time: 5 minutes

2½ cups (600ml) chicken stock
(page 35)

2 tablespoons (25g) butter

3 tablespoons (20g) all-purpose
(plain) flour

Salt and freshly ground black
pepper

Gravy is, of course, the classic accompaniment to roast chicken. You can use the same method for making gravy for any roast meat.

Once the chicken is cooked and removed from the roasting pan to rest and keep warm (see page 96), place the pan over medium heat and deglaze with a little of the stock, stirring with a wooden spoon and scraping any sticky bits from the bottom of the pan.

Drain off the fat using a separating pitcher or, if you don't have one, pour the liquid into a bowl and add a handful of ice cubes. After a few minutes, the fat will float to the surface. Remove and discard the fat; pour the remaining liquid into a saucepan with the remaining chicken stock over medium heat.

To make a roux, melt the butter in a medium-size saucepan over medium heat. Add the flour, stirring, and allow it to cook for 2 minutes, then remove from the heat.

Bring the stock and pan juices to a boil, whisk in the roux a little at a time, and continue to boil for 2 to 3 minutes to thicken very slightly. Season to taste with salt and pepper. Just before serving the chicken, strain the gravy through a fine sieve into a gravy boat or pitcher.

Tarragon cream sauce

Makes about 1 cup (250 ml)

Preparation time: 5 minutes

Cooking time: 5 minutes

2½ cups (600ml) chicken stock (page 35)

½ cup (100ml) heavy or whipping (double or regular) cream

2 tablespoons chopped fresh tarragon

2 tablespoons (25g) butter (optional)

3 tablespoons (20g) all-purpose (plain) flour (optional)

This is particularly good with roast chicken made with the Smoked Bacon Stuffing (page 161). The recipe assumes you have just roasted a chicken.

Once the chicken is cooked and removed from the roasting pan to rest and keep warm (see page 96), place the pan over medium heat and deglaze with a little of the stock, stirring with a wooden spoon and scraping any sticky bits from the bottom of the pan.

Drain off the fat using a separating pitcher or, if you don't have one, pour the pan juice into a bowl and add a handful of ice cubes. After a few minutes, the fat will float to the surface. Remove and discard the fat; pour the remaining pan juices into a saucepan with the remaining chicken stock.

Bring the stock and juices to a boil over medium heat and add the cream and tarragon. Simmer for 3 to 4 minutes, uncovered, stirring regularly, until reduced and thickened. If you'd like it even thicker you can use a roux. To make the roux, melt the butter in a medium-size saucepan over medium heat. Add the flour, stirring, and allow it to cook for 2 minutes, then remove from the heat. Whisk the roux into the tarragon sauce, a little at a time, over low heat.

Chicken open-pot roast

Serves 4

Preparation time: 10 minutes

Cooking time: 35 to 40 minutes

3 tablespoons extra virgin olive oil

1 chicken, cut into pieces, or 4 chicken thighs or breasts (with the skin left on)

Salt and freshly ground black pepper

1 pound (450g) new potatoes (unpeeled), larger ones halved

2 small leeks or 1 large leek, trimmed and cut into 1-inch (3cm) lengths

1 cup (250ml) chicken stock (page 35)

1 sprig of tarragon, plus 1 tablespoon chopped fresh tarragon

4 tablespoons freshly squeezed lemon juice

1 tablespoon Dijon mustard

It's at the end of May that the first of the new season's potatoes begin to appear. We Irish adore spuds, and each year brings such excitement because there is just nothing quite like a freshly dug new potato, be it from a local farm or, even better, from your own garden.

This dish is my light and summery take on chicken casserole. Cooked in an open pot, the chicken skin is allowed to get golden and crisp, but there is still plenty of delicious sauce, which the new potatoes readily soak up. Serve with a green salad.

Preheat the oven to 425°F (220°C/Gas mark 7).

Pour the olive oil into a Dutch oven or a large, wide flameproof casserole dish over high heat. Season the chicken pieces with salt and pepper and place, skin side down, in the hot oil. Cook for 4 to 5 minutes, until a deep golden brown. Turn over, so that the skin side is now on top. Add the potatoes and leeks, season with salt and pepper, and gently stir for another 2 minutes, being careful to keep the chicken skin side up. Pour in the stock and add the sprig of tarragon. Bring to a boil.

Transfer to the oven, uncovered, and bake for about 30 minutes, or until the potatoes are tender and the chicken is cooked through. Remove from the oven, stir in the chopped tarragon along with the lemon juice and mustard, and serve immediately.

Roast duck with potato stuffing

Serves 4

Preparation time: 10 minutes

Cooking time: 2 hours

1 whole duck (about 4 pounds/1.8kg)

Salt and freshly ground black pepper

FOR THE STUFFING

1 tablespoon (15g) butter

½ onion (about 4 ounces/125g), chopped

1 cup (125g) peeled and chopped tart apple

1 large baking or russet (floury) potato (8 ounces/225g), unpeeled

1 teaspoon finely grated orange zest

2 teaspoons fresh thyme leaves, chopped

Salt and freshly ground black pepper

FOR THE GRAVY

1¼ cups (300ml) chicken stock (page 35) or duck stock

2 tablespoons (25g) butter

3 tablespoons (20g) all-purpose (plain) flour

Duck is a bird rich with flavor and a divine coating of glorious fat. Cooking duck means taking advantage of that wonderful fat and a potato stuffing is perfect. The mashed potato and apple soaks up all those delicious juices, just as stuffing should!

A golden, crisp-skinned duck makes a magnificent centerpiece. Serve with Granny's Roasted Herbed Potatoes (page 158), Sticky Cumin and Apricot Roast Carrots and Parsnips (page 155), and Buttered Cabbage (page 144).

First make the stuffing. Melt the butter in a saucepan over medium heat. When the butter foams, add the onion and apple. Decrease the heat to low, cover, and sweat for 7 to 10 minutes, until soft. Remove from the heat.

While the onions and apples are cooking, start cooking the potato. Put the potato in a large saucepan of cold water with a good pinch of salt. Bring to a boil and cook for 10 minutes, then pour all but about 1½ inches (4cm) of the water out of the pan and continue to cook the potato over very low heat. (Don't be tempted to stick a knife into it because the skin will break, and the potato will just disintegrate and get soggy if you do.)

About 20 minutes later, when you think the potato might be cooked, test with a skewer; if the potato is soft, take it off the heat. Peel the potato while still hot and mash immediately; add to the apple and onion mixture. Stir in the orange zest and thyme and season with salt and pepper. Allow to get quite cool before stuffing your duck.

Preheat the oven to 350°F (180°C/Gas mark 4).

Season the cavity of the duck with salt and pepper and spoon in the stuffing. Place the duck on a rack in a roasting pan and pierce the skin all over with the point of a sharp knife (this will help release the fat during cooking). Season the skin well, particularly with salt, to help crisp it up during cooking.

Roast for about 1½ hours, allowing about 20 minutes per pound (450g), basting occasionally and draining any excess fat from the pan. When the duck is cooked, the legs should feel slightly loose and a metal skewer inserted into the thigh should be too hot to hold

recipe continues overleaf

against the inside of your wrist. When cooked, transfer the duck to a serving plate and leave to rest, covered with aluminum foil, in the oven at the lowest temperature, if possible, while you make the gravy.

Drain any fat from the roasting pan using a fat separator (separating jug) or, if you don't have one, pour the liquid from the pan into a bowl and add a handful of ice cubes. After a few minutes the fat will float to the surface. Remove and discard the fat (saving, if you wish, for roast potatoes on another day), then pour the remaining cooking juices into a saucepan.

To make the gravy, first make a roux. Melt the butter in a medium-size saucepan over medium heat. Add the flour, stirring, and allow it to cook for 2 minutes, then remove from the heat. Set aside. Place the roasting pan over medium heat and deglaze with a little of the cooking juices or stock, stirring with a wooden spoon and scraping any sticky bits from the bottom of the pan. Pour this into the saucepan with the cooking juices, add the remaining stock, and bring to a boil. Whisk in the roux, a little at a time, and continue to boil for 2 to 3 minutes to thicken to the desired consistency. Season to taste with salt and pepper, if necessary. Just before serving, strain the gravy through a fine sieve into a warm gravy boat or pitcher.

Spoon the stuffing out of the duck into a serving bowl or onto a serving plate. Carve the duck breasts away from the carcass and cut each one in half. Remove the leg portions and divide them in half, too. Serve a breast and leg portion to each person, along with some stuffing and gravy.

Pot-roasted duck legs with onions and root vegetables

Serves 4

Preparation time: 10 minutes

Cooking time: 1 to 1½ hours

1½ teaspoons extra virgin olive oil

4 duck legs, excess fat removed, but with the skin left on

4 onions, halved through the root, each half cut lengthwise into 4 wedges

4 sprigs of rosemary

Salt and freshly ground black pepper

6 baking or russet (floury) potatoes, peeled and cut into ¾-inch (2cm) dice

6 small white turnips, peeled and cut into ½- to ¾-inch (1–2cm) dice

This is the food I love to serve on a wintery weekend evening when friends are over. It's a dish for an easy-going dinner party, to serve with plenty of red wine and lots of laughter.

Turnips are eaten less around the world, but we still eat them here in Ireland. There are large sweet turnips, but I prefer the small white ones because they're more refined in flavor and are particularly at home with duck or goose.

Preheat the oven to 400°F (200°C/Gas mark 6).

Heat the olive oil in a Dutch oven or flameproof casserole dish over medium heat. Add the duck legs, skin side down, followed by the onions, rosemary, and salt and pepper. Cook for 4 to 5 minutes, until the skin is a rich golden brown. Tip in the potatoes and turnips and cover with a lid.

Roast in the oven for 1 to 1¼ hours, by which time the onions should be golden and the root vegetables and duck cooked through and tender.

Irish weekend fry-up

Serves 1

Preparation time: 10 minutes

Cooking time: 25 minutes

Vegetable, sunflower, or olive oil, for frying

Butter, for frying and spreading on toast

1–2 medium-size pork sausages

1–2 slices (rashers) thick-cut, dry-cured, smoked or unsmoked, Canadian (back) or regular (streaky) bacon, rind removed

2 to 3 slices of black and/or white pudding

2 ounces (50g) button mushrooms, sliced, or 1 large flat mushroom, stem removed

Salt and freshly ground black pepper

1 ripe tomato, halved

Pinch of sugar (if roasting the tomato in the oven)

FOR THE EGGS

1 to 2 eggs

½ tablespoon milk (for scrambled eggs)

1 to 1½ tablespoons (15–20g) butter (for scrambled eggs)

2 slices white or whole-grain (brown) bread

A fry-up is great when friends are staying over—simply multiply the ingredients given below by however many people you are feeding. Source the best local ingredients you can and follow up with a big walk. You can have your eggs boiled or poached, if you prefer.

Our family eats an Irish breakfast or some parts of it at least once a week, and not always in the morning. We're lucky to have great producers of bacon and, of course, black and white pudding, which is a particular specialty of Cork County. Black pudding (blood sausage) may be more popular worldwide, but white pudding is very popular in Ireland and an important part of an Irish breakfast. White pudding is similar to black pudding, but it contains no blood—only pork, spices, and usually oatmeal. I love this big cooked breakfast, but it isn't something I'll eat early in the morning before I go for a run!

Heat 1 tablespoon oil and 1 tablespoon butter in a large frying pan over medium heat. Add the sausages and fry for 10 to 15 minutes, until golden and cooked through. Add the bacon and fry for 3 to 4 minutes on each side, until crisp and golden, dabbing off any milky liquid with paper towels. Add the black and/or white pudding slices to the pan and fry for 2 to 3 minutes on each side, until beginning to crisp; the white pudding (if using) should turn golden. Remove the sausages, bacon, and pudding slices from the pan and drain on paper towels.

Place in an ovenproof dish in a low oven to keep warm.

Meanwhile, add a dash of oil and pat (knob) of butter to another frying pan over medium heat. Add the button mushrooms and sauté for 3 to 4 minutes, until softened and turning golden. Season with salt and pepper, then remove from the pan and keep warm (adding to the dish with the sausages and bacon). If you are cooking a large flat mushroom, then add the oil and butter to the pan and fry the mushroom for 8 to 10 minutes, turning halfway through, until softened and browned.

Season the cut side of the tomato halves with salt and pepper and drizzle over 1 tablespoon of oil. Gently fry them, cut side down first, for 2 to 3 minutes, then turn over and fry for another 2 to 3 minutes, until just softened.

recipe continues overleaf

Alternatively, cook the large flat mushroom and/or the tomatoes in the oven. Preheat the oven to 400°F (200°C/ Gas mark 6). Drizzle 2 teaspoons of olive oil over or add a pat (knob) of butter to the mushroom and season with salt and pepper before roasting for 12 to 15 minutes until tender. Put a pat (knob) of butter on the cut side of each tomato half, add the sugar, and season with a little salt and pepper before roasting for 12 to 15 minutes, until softened. If you are using the oven, begin roasting the mushroom and tomatoes a few minutes before frying the sausages and bacon. Once cooked, decrease the oven temperature to low for keeping everything warm as it is cooked.

To fry an egg, melt a pat (knob) of butter in a small, clean frying pan over low heat. Carefully crack the egg into the pan and allow to fry gently. For an over-easy egg, fry for 1 to 2 minutes, until it begins to set, then flip over and fry for another 1 to 2 minutes. If you prefer your egg sunny side up, then fry gently for 4 to 5 minutes, until the yolk has filmed over. Remove from the pan and serve immediately with the other cooked ingredients.

For scrambled eggs, crack the eggs into a bowl, add the milk, season with salt and pepper, and beat together. Add 1 tablespoon of the butter to a small saucepan over low heat. Immediately pour in the eggs and cook for 2 to 3 minutes, stirring continuously (I find a wooden spatula best for this), until the butter has melted and the eggs are softly scrambled. Remove from the heat immediately so that the eggs don't become overcooked. Serve with the other cooked ingredients.

While the egg is cooking, put the slices of bread in a toaster or toast under a preheated broiler (grill) for a few minutes (and on both sides, if using the broiler/grill) until golden. Butter the toast and cut the slices in half.

To serve, arrange everything on a warm serving plate, with the hot buttered toast on the side and with some tomato ketchup (see opposite) or relish.

Rachel's ketchup

Vegetarian

Makes about ¾ cup (200 ml)

Preparation time: 10 minutes

Cooking time: 1 hour 10 minutes

2 tablespoons extra virgin olive oil

8 ounces (225g) onions, coarsely chopped

3⅔ cups (650g) coarsely chopped tomatoes (about 6 small to medium tomatoes)

2 cloves garlic, crushed or finely grated

6 tablespoons white wine vinegar

⅓ cup (75g) superfine (caster) or granulated sugar

2 teaspoons Dijon mustard

Pinch of ground allspice

Pinch of ground cloves

½ teaspoon salt

½ teaspoon freshly ground black pepper

If your children regularly eat ketchup, then you might want them to try this delicious and much healthier homemade version. If you think they won't take to it, ease them into it by mixing some into their usual brand and gradually adjusting their taste. This is definitely best made in the summer with lovely ripe red tomatoes. It keeps for many weeks in the fridge because of the vinegar and sugar. It's possible to freeze the sauce—perhaps as ice cubes for speedy thawing.

Heat the olive oil in a saucepan over medium heat. Add the onions and sauté for 8 to 10 minutes, until softened and a little golden. Add the tomatoes, garlic, white wine vinegar, sugar, mustard, allspice, cloves, salt, and pepper. Cover with a lid and simmer for about 30 minutes, or until very soft.

Remove from the heat and purée in a food processor or using a handheld blender. Pour through a sieve into a clean saucepan and simmer, uncovered and stirring regularly, for another 30 minutes, or until the mixture is thick.

Pour into sterilized jars and store in the fridge (see Rachel's tip on page 188).

Bacon and cabbage with parsley sauce

Serves 6

Preparation time: 20 minutes

Cooking time: 1½ hours

2-pound (900g) piece back bacon or cured and smoked pork loin (loin or collar of bacon)

1 small Savoy cabbage, outer leaves removed

2 tablespoons (25g) butter

Salt and freshly ground black pepper

FOR THE PARSLEY SAUCE

1¼ cups (300ml) Basic White Sauce (page 114)

1 teaspoon Dijon mustard

7 tablespoons (25g) finely chopped fresh parsley

Salt and freshly ground black pepper

This is a traditional Irish dish in which the cabbage is boiled in the water used for cooking the bacon. Many people recall it with affection, while others remember it for the overcooked cabbage. Providing the cabbage is cooked for only 3 to 5 minutes, you won't be disappointed. This dish is also delicious served with Creamy Mashed Potato (see page 166), or boiled or baked potatoes, and some hot mustard.

Put the bacon in a large saucepan, cover with water, and bring slowly to a boil. Drain, refill the pan with fresh water, and repeat. This is to get rid of the salt (which appears as white froth on top of the water), so it may need to be done again, depending how salty the bacon is. Taste the water to check for saltiness and keep checking and boiling again in fresh water until you are happy with the flavor.

Cover with fresh hot water and bring to a boil for the final time. Decrease the heat, cover with a lid, and simmer for about 40 minutes (allowing 20 minutes per pound/450g), occasionally skimming any sediment that rises to the surface. Once the bacon is cooked (a skewer inserted in the middle should come out easily), remove from the pan (reserving the cooking liquid) and let rest, covered with foil, a clean kitchen towel, or upturned bowl.

In the meantime, prepare the parsley sauce. Make the white sauce following the instructions on page 114, then stir in the mustard and parsley. Check the seasoning and adjust if necessary. Cover and keep warm in the pan.

Cut the cabbage into quarters, remove the core, and finely shred across the grain. Bring the cooking liquid for the bacon to a fast boil. Add the cabbage and cook for about 3 minutes, until just tender (it's easy to overcook). Drain well, squeezing out any excess water, and return to the saucepan. Add the butter to the cabbage, tossing to melt, and season to taste with salt and pepper.

Remove and discard the rind from the bacon, if necessary, and slice the bacon into thick pieces. Serve the bacon with the buttered cabbage and parsley sauce.

Basic white sauce

Vegetarian

Makes about 1¼ cups (300ml)

Preparation time: 5 minutes

Cooking time: 20 minutes

1¼ cups (300ml) whole milk

Few slices of carrot

Few slices of onion

1 sprig of parsley

1 sprig of thyme

3 peppercorns

2 tablespoons (15g) all-purpose
(plain) flour

1 tablespoon (15g) butter

Salt and freshly ground black
pepper

This makes a sauce thick enough to coat the back of a spoon. It is thickened using a roux, which is made from flour and butter cooked together. If you would like a thicker sauce, use twice as much butter and flour when making your roux.

Pour the milk into a small saucepan and add the carrot, onion, parsley, thyme, and peppercorns. Bring to a boil, decrease the heat, and simmer for 4 to 5 minutes. Remove from the heat and leave to infuse for about 10 minutes.

While the milk infuses, make the roux. Melt the butter in a small saucepan over low to medium heat and add the flour. Allow to cook for 2 minutes, stirring regularly. Set aside.

Strain the milk through a sieve placed over a small saucepan and bring the milk to a boil. Whisk in the roux, a little at a time, until well blended and allow to simmer gently for 4 to 5 minutes, or until thickened to the desired consistency. Season to taste and use as a plain white sauce or add your choice of flavoring.

Rachel's tip
For a speedier version, melt the butter in a large saucepan on medium heat and add the flour, stirring for a few seconds. Take off the heat and gradually add the milk, stirring continuously until the milk is fully incorporated and the sauce is lump free. Return the pan to gentle heat and cook the sauce for 6 to 8 minutes, stirring constantly, until thickened and smooth.

Crumbed bacon chops with sweet whiskey sauce

Serves 4 to 6

Preparation time: 10 minutes

Cooking time: 1¼ hours

2-pound (900g) piece back bacon, unsmoked

1 cup (110g) all-purpose (plain) flour

1 egg

2½ cups (110g) fresh white bread crumbs

Salt and freshly ground black pepper

2 tablespoons (25g) butter

1 tablespoon extra virgin olive oil

FOR THE WHISKEY SAUCE

1 cup (225g) sugar

6 tablespoons cold water

¼ cup (50ml) hot water

3 to 4 tablespoons Irish whiskey

This is a dish often made at Ballymaloe. I adore the crispy coating around the bacon chops and the way the sweetness of the sauce combines perfectly with the saltiness of the bacon. Serve with some vegetables and boiled new potatoes or Creamy Mashed Potatoes (page 166). If you're feeding children, leave the whiskey out of the sauce because the alcohol does not burn off. Substitute orange or pineapple juice.

Put the bacon in a large saucepan, cover with water, and bring slowly to a boil. Drain, refill the pan with fresh water, and repeat. This is to get rid of the salt (which appears as white froth on top of the water), so it may need to be done again, depending how salty the bacon is. Taste the water to check for saltiness and keep checking and boiling again in fresh water until you are happy with the flavor.

Cover with fresh hot water and bring to a boil for the final time. Decrease the heat, cover with a lid, and simmer for about 40 minutes (allowing 20 minutes per pound/450g), occasionally skimming any sediment that rises to the surface. Once the bacon is cooked (a skewer inserted in the middle should come out easily), lift out of the water, drain well, and allow to cool a little.

Meanwhile, prepare the sauce. Put the sugar in a saucepan with the cold water and bring slowly to a boil over low heat, stirring until the sugar dissolves. Boil without stirring for about 10 minutes, until it turns a chestnut-brown color, swirling the pan to caramelize evenly. Remove from the heat and immediately add the hot water. Stir to make a smooth sauce, then add the whiskey. Keep warm in the pan.

Sift the flour into a wide shallow bowl, beat the egg in a small bowl, put the bread crumbs in a third dish, and season all three with salt and pepper. Remove the bacon rind (if not already removed), and slice into chops ½ to ¾ inch (1–2cm) thick. Dip each chop first in the flour, then in the egg, and finally in the bread crumbs to coat.

Combine the butter and oil in a large frying pan over medium heat. When the butter starts to froth, fry the chops for 3 to 4 minutes on each side, until crisp and golden. Serve the crumbed bacon chops with the sweet whiskey sauce drizzled over.

Kinoith pork casserole

Serves 6 to 8

Preparation time: 20 minutes

Cooking time: 2 hours

3⅓ pounds (1.5kg) bone-in shoulder pork chops, cut about ½ inch (1cm) thick

3 tablespoons extra virgin olive oil

Salt and freshly ground black pepper

12 pearl or boiling onions, peeled (see tip), or 3 to 4 cooking onions, cut into quarters lengthwise through the root

3 carrots, thickly sliced, or 12 baby carrots, scrubbed and left whole

3-inch (8cm) piece of fresh ginger, peeled and finely grated

4¼ cups (1l) chicken stock (page 35)

3 pounds (1.3kg) potatoes (about 12 small), peeled and halved if large

3 tablespoons chopped fresh cilantro (coriander)

My father-in-law Timmy created this recipe, and we eat it regularly. The ginger flavor is quite subtle, so feel free to increase the amount, if you wish. If you use loin chops, there is probably no need to remove any fat after cooking.

Preheat the oven to 325°F (170°C/Gas mark 3).

Cut the pork chops in half without removing the bones because they will greatly add to the flavor. Heat the olive oil in a Dutch oven or flameproof casserole dish with a tight-fitting lid over high heat. When the oil is really hot, add the meat in batches, searing the chops for about 1 minute on each side, or until golden brown, seasoning with salt and pepper as it cooks. Remove from the pan and set aside.

Add the onions and carrots to the hot oil and sauté for 3 to 4 minutes, until soft; season with salt and pepper. Return the chops to the pan. Add the ginger, pour in the stock, and bring to a boil. Put the potatoes on top of the chops, cover with a lid, and bake for 1½ to 1¾ hours, until the meat is very tender and the sauce has thickened slightly.

Once cooked, strain the stew through a colander over a large bowl to catch the cooking liquid. Return the meat and vegetables to the pan with the lid on to keep warm and let the liquid stand for a minute or so to allow the fat to float to the top (adding some ice cubes will help speed up the cooling process). Remove the fat with a spoon and return the liquid to the pan. Warm through over low heat, stir in the cilantro, and serve.

Rachel's tips
You can replace the olive oil with 3 tablespoons of fat rendered from the pork. Heat any pork fat trimmings from the meat in a small saucepan until melted to a liquid.

If the potatoes are quite small, add them to the dish 20 to 30 minutes after the stew starts cooking to prevent them from breaking up.

To quickly peel the pearl onions, place them in a bowl, cover with boiling water, and allow to stand for a few minutes before draining. The skins should then peel off very easily.

Slow-roasted shoulder of pork

Serves 6 to 8

Preparation time: 15 minutes

Cooking time: 6 hours 20 minutes

6- to 8-pound (3–4kg) bone-in pork shoulder or Boston butt

Salt and freshly ground black pepper

1 bulb garlic, broken up into cloves (unpeeled)

1 butternut squash (about 2 pounds/ 900g) with skin, seeded and cut into ½- to ¾-inch (1–2cm) cubes

4 trimmed leeks (about 13 ounces/ 375g in total), cut into ½-inch (1cm) thick slices

Small handful of sage leaves

I love that with this gorgeous dish you simply put the pork in the oven in the morning, then carry on with your day. By dinnertime you'll have the most succulent and tender piece of meat. The shoulder is one of the cheaper cuts of pork and, when cooked correctly, it is definitely my favorite. It demands to be cooked slowly, allowing the fat to melt and moisten the meat and giving the flavors time to develop. When this pork is ready, it is so tender you don't need to carve it into slices, and nor would you be able to. Just pull off succulent shreds of the meat and pieces of crispy crackling and serve with the roasted vegetables.

Preheat the oven to 425°F (220°C/Gas mark 7).

Using a sharp knife, score the rind of the pork in a crisscross pattern at ¼-inch (5mm) intervals, cutting through the fat but not into the meat itself. (Or ask your butcher to do this for you, if you prefer.) Sprinkle over 1 tablespoon of salt, rubbing it into the lines scored in the fat, place the pork in a large roasting pan, and roast in the oven for 30 minutes. Decrease the temperature to 300°F (150°C/Gas mark 2) and continue to cook for another 5 hours.

Remove the pork from the oven and turn the temperature up to 425°F (220°C/Gas mark 7). Pour off the fat into a bowl, leaving any juices in the pan. Place the garlic, squash, leeks, and sage leaves around the pork. Then pour over 3 tablespoons of the reserved fat, season with salt and pepper, and toss the vegetables together in the pan. Return to the oven for 40 to 50 minutes, until the pork rind has turned into delicious crackling, and the vegetables are cooked through and golden. Serve from the pan or transfer to a large plate.

Roast pork belly with a cumin and garlic rub

Serves 4 to 6

Preparation time: 10 minutes

Cooking time: 3¾ to 4¼ hours

About 3⅓ pounds (1.5kg) pork belly, rind left on

1¼ cups (300ml) chicken stock (page 35)

Salt and freshly ground black pepper

FOR THE CUMIN AND GARLIC RUB

2 tablespoons cumin seeds, toasted and ground

6 cloves garlic, peeled

2 teaspoons salt

2 to 3 tablespoons extra virgin olive oil

Pork belly is the perfect expression of pork, with just the right amount of wonderfully flavorful fat, which not only tastes fabulous but also keeps the meat incredibly moist. Belly needs to cook for quite a long time in order for (nearly) all the fat to come out and for the crackling to become deliciously crisp and crunchy. Make sure that the rind is still on when you buy it (it's essential for the crackling!). Serve with Root Vegetable Mash (page 165) and Buttered Cabbage (page 144).

Preheat the oven to 300°F (150°C/Gas mark 2).

For the rub, combine the cumin, garlic, and salt and whiz everything together using a handheld blender, or just finely chop everything by hand and mix together well in a bowl. Add enough olive oil to form a coarse paste.

Score the rind on the pork belly, using a very sharp knife and making long cuts through the rind and into the fat (but not into the meat), from one side of the fat to the other at roughly ¼-inch (5mm) intervals.

Massage the paste into the scored lines in the rind and place the meat rind side up in a roasting pan. Roast in the oven for 3½ to 4 hours, until the meat is very tender (you should be able to cut the meat with a spoon). Turn up the heat to 425°F (220°C/Gas mark 7), and roast for another 10 to 15 minutes, until the rind is crisp and crackly.

Transfer the pork to a serving plate, and allow to rest in the oven, with the heat turned off, or somewhere warm for at least 15 minutes.

While the pork is resting, make the gravy. Pour off any excess fat from the roasting pan, then place the pan over medium heat, and deglaze by pouring in the stock, whisking continuously to dissolve the caramelized juices sticking to the bottom of the pan. Pour the juices into a separating pitcher or pour the liquid into a bowl and skim off the melted fat from the surface. It can help to add a few ice cubes; the fat will solidify and float to the surface after a few minutes, and you can then scoop it out and discard it.

Return the meat juices to a small saucepan, bring to a boil, season with salt and pepper, if necessary, then pour into a pitcher to serve straight away or reheat when you are ready to serve.

Carve the pork into slices and serve with the gravy.

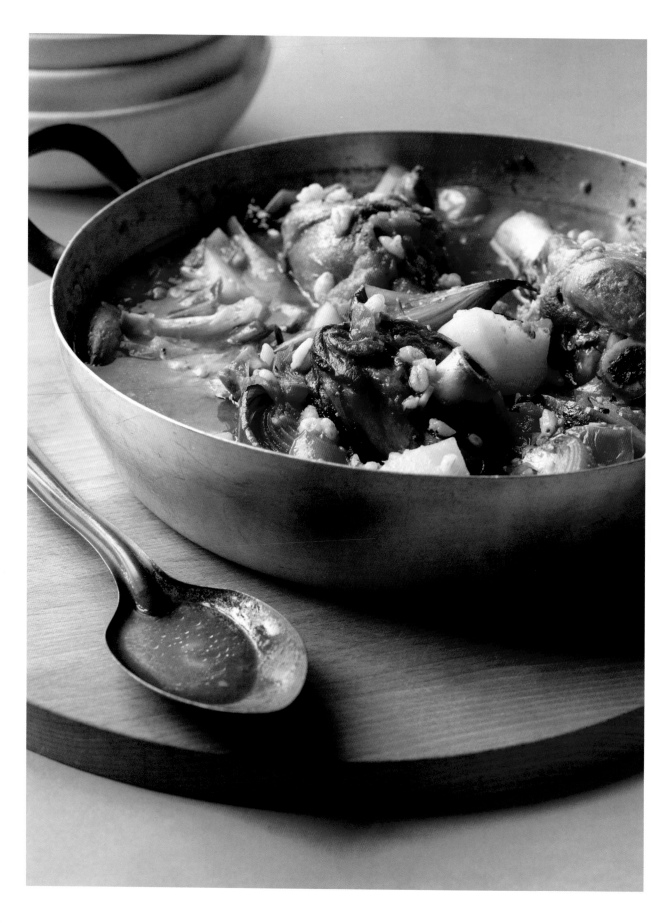

Lamb shanks with potatoes and pearl barley

Serves 4

Preparation time: 10 to 15 minutes

Cooking time: 3½ hours

2 tablespoons extra virgin olive oil

4 lamb shanks

Salt and freshly ground black pepper

4 red onions, cut lengthwise through the root end into 6 wedges

4 cloves garlic, finely chopped

4 tomatoes, cut into 1-inch (3cm) chunks

1 teaspoon sugar

4 tablespoons (50g) pearl barley

2 cups (500ml) chicken stock (page 35)

About 3 pounds (1.3kg) baking or russet (floury) potatoes, peeled and quartered

Every August for a few years running, I cooked for a wonderful American couple who owned a house in Ireland. On dull rainy days they would request this most comforting dish. It's very convenient to make because most of the ingredients just go into the pot together, and the only thing you have to think about after that is adding the potatoes.

Preheat the oven to 300°F (150°C/Gas mark 2).

Pour the olive oil into a Dutch oven or flameproof casserole dish over medium-high heat. Season the lamb shanks with salt and pepper. When the oil is hot, add the shanks and cook for about 4 minutes on each side, or until they begin to brown. Add the onions, garlic, tomatoes, sugar, pearl barley, and chicken stock. Bring to a boil, then cover with a lid, and bake in the oven for 2½ hours.

Add the potatoes, cover again, and return to the oven for another 50 to 60 minutes, until the potatoes are cooked and the lamb shanks meltingly tender.

Leg of lamb with roasted vegetables

Serves 6 to 8

Preparation time: 15 minutes

Cooking time: 1¾ to 2 hours

1 leg of lamb (6½ to 8¾ pounds/3–4kg) bone in

Salt and freshly ground black pepper

1½ pounds (750g) baking or russet (floury) potatoes, peeled and cut into ⅜-inch (7mm) slices

3 parsnips (about 1 pound/450g in total), peeled and cut into ⅜-inch (7mm) slices

3 red onions, cut lengthwise through the root end into ½-inch (1cm) wedges

1 tablespoon fresh thyme leaves or chopped rosemary leaves

3 tablespoons extra virgin olive oil

Red Currant Jelly (page 128) or Mint Sauce (page 128), to serve

A Sunday roast can sometimes take some time to put together and to coordinate all the side dishes. This recipe avoids that altogether because the lamb is cooked on a rack over the vegetables allowing them to soak up all the juices and flavor of the meat and saving you time cooking and clearing up! When you are buying the leg of lamb, ask your butcher to remove the aitchbone at the top of the leg and trim the knuckle from the end.

Preheat the oven to 350°F (180°C/Gas mark 4).

If necessary, remove the papery skin from the lamb. Then, using a sharp knife, make long shallow scores in a crisscross pattern in the fat, spacing the lines 1 inch (3cm) apart, and season well with salt and pepper.

Combine the potatoes, parsnips, onions, thyme, and olive oil in a large roasting pan and toss together, seasoning with salt and pepper. Spread everything out in the pan and place the lamb on a rack over the top (if you don't have a rack, place the lamb in the roasting pan and surround it with the vegetables). Roast for 1½ hours, or until the lamb is cooked to your desire.

Remove the pan from the oven and increase the heat to 425°F (220°C/Gas mark 7). Transfer the lamb to a large plate or a board sitting in a tray, cover with aluminum foil, and leave to rest somewhere warm.

Put the vegetables back in the oven and roast for another 20 to 30 minutes, or until golden on top.

About 10 minutes before the vegetables are ready, start carving the lamb. Then divide among plates, adding spoonfuls of the vegetables, and serve with red currant jelly or mint sauce.

Red currant jelly

Vegetarian

Makes 3 half-pint (300ml) jars

Preparation time: 5 minutes

Cooking time: 10 minutes

18 ounces (500g) fresh or frozen (and defrosted) red currants, stems removed

2½ cups (500g) granulated or superfine (caster) sugar

Delicious with roast meat, especially lamb (see page 126), this will keep for months in sterilized jars in the fridge. Use frozen red currants instead of fresh, if necessary.

Combine the red currants and sugar in a large, heavy saucepan and stir over medium heat until the sugar dissolves and the mixture comes to a boil. Increase the heat and boil for 6 minutes, stirring every now and then to prevent it from sticking to the bottom of the pan. Spoon off any froth that has come to the top.

Pour the mixture into a nonreactive sieve. Allow it to drip through without pushing it with a spoon (which will cause the jelly to become cloudy) and then place in clean, sterilized jars (see Rachel's tip on page 188).

Mint sauce

Vegetarian

Makes ⅓ cup (75ml)

Preparation time: 10 minutes

3 tablespoons chopped fresh mint

1 heaping tablespoon granulated or superfine (caster) sugar

¼ cup (50ml) boiling water

1 tablespoon freshly squeezed lemon juice or white wine vinegar

The classic accompaniment to roast lamb (see page 126), mint sauce is best made on the day, up to a couple of hours before serving.

Combine the mint and sugar in a small bowl and pour over the boiling water. Stir to dissolve the sugar, then stir in the lemon juice. Let stand for at least 10 minutes before serving.

Beef and red wine hot pot

Serves 6

Preparation time: 15 minutes

Cooking time: 2½ hours

3 to 4 tablespoons extra virgin olive oil

9 ounces (250g) button mushrooms, halved (or quartered if they are large)

Salt and freshly ground black pepper

2 small onions, sliced

4 cloves garlic, finely chopped

3⅓ pounds (1.5kg) stewing beef, cut into 2-inch (6cm) chunks

⅔ cup (150ml) red wine

1 tablespoon chopped fresh thyme leaves

1 tablespoon red wine vinegar

1½ pounds (650g) baking or russet (floury) potatoes, peeled and cut into ¼-inch (5mm) slices

2 tablespoons (25g) butter, diced

This is just the sort of rich and warming dish that is so popular in Ireland. It must be all the cold weather and, of course, all the rain. We shouldn't complain too much about the rain, because it's what makes the grass so green and produces such delicious and full-flavored beef. Here, stewing cuts of beef are cooked long and slow with a full-bodied red wine and covered by potatoes, making this dish a convenient one-pot supper. You can even prepare it in advance and keep covered, in the fridge, for up to 24 hours before cooking.

Preheat the oven to 300°F (150°C/Gas mark 2).

Heat 3 tablespoons of the olive oil in a Dutch oven or flameproof casserole dish over medium-high heat. Add the mushrooms, season with salt and pepper, and toss for 2 to 3 minutes, until lightly golden. Remove the mushrooms from the pan with a slotted spoon and set aside.

If there isn't much oil left in the dish or pan, add another tablespoon. Tip in the onions and garlic, stir over the heat, season with salt and pepper, and cook for 4 to 5 minutes, until they start to turn golden at the edges. Add the meat and wine and 2 teaspoons of the thyme leaves. Bring to a boil and cover with a lid.

Bake in the oven for 1¼ to 1½ hours, until the meat is just tender. Take the pan out of the oven and turn up the heat to 450°F (230°C/Gas mark 8). Stir in the mushrooms and red wine vinegar. Arrange the potato slices over the beef in the pan (it's fine if there's more than one layer). Scatter over the remaining 1 teaspoon thyme and some salt and pepper, then dot with the butter.

Return the Dutch oven to the (now hot) oven and bake for another 30 to 40 minutes, or until the potatoes are cooked through and beginning to turn golden. Bring to the table and serve.

Ballymaloe spiced beef

Serves 12 to 16

Preparation time: 20 minutes (plus 3 to 7 days to cure)

Cooking time: 2 to 3 hours

About 4¼ pounds (2kg) beef bottom round, rump roast, or silverside of beef

BALLYMALOE SPICE MIXTURE

½ cup (100g) Demerara or light brown sugar

½ cup (125g) salt

¾ teaspoon (5g) pink salt (sodium nitrate also called Prague powder)

2 tablespoons plus 1 teaspoon (25g) whole black peppercorns

4 tablespoons (25g) whole allspice (pimento or Jamaican pepper)

4 tablespoons (25g) whole juniper berries

Cucumber Pickles (page 133), to serve

Tomato Relish (page 20), to serve

Spiced beef used to be eaten all over Ireland at Christmas and New Year. In Cork, however, we eat spiced beef all year round, and it is sold daily at the city's famous English Market. This spiced beef recipe has been passed down the Allen family, and I think it's absolutely divine. In fact the first time I had spiced beef was when I came from Dublin to do the Cookery Course at Ballymaloe.

Spiced beef is useful to have in the fridge; it lasts for up to 6 weeks and is delicious thinly sliced and served with a little pickle and chutney. This recipe makes enough spice for this amount of beef. But if you have a smaller piece of beef, then use half of the mixture and keep the rest in a jar for 3 months.

Make the spice mixture by grinding all the ingredients (preferably in a spice grinder in a few batches) until fairly fine.

To prepare the beef, remove any bones and trim off any large pieces of fat (do keep some of the fat). Place the beef in an earthenware dish and rub the spice into every crevice of the beef. Leave in the fridge for 3 to 7 days, depending on the thickness of the meat. Turn it occasionally. (This is a dry spice, but after 1 to 2 days some liquid will come out of the meat.) The longer the meat is left in the spice, the longer it will last and the stronger the spiced flavor.

Jut before cooking the meat, roll and tie the meat neatly with cotton string into a compact shape, place in a large saucepan, cover with cold water, and simmer for 2 to 3 hours (about 20 minutes per pound /450g) or until soft and cooked. When cooked you should be able to insert a skewer into the center, and the skewer will come out easily.

If you're serving the beef warm, remove from the liquid, then place on a carving board, cut away the string, and carve into slices to serve. If the beef is to be eaten cold, remove it from the liquid, place in a high-sided pan, such as a roasting pan or gratin dish, cover it with a chopping board, and weigh it down with four or five cans of tomatoes or beans (or something of a similar weight) and leave for 12 hours. After 12 hours, remove the board and weights. It will now keep in the fridge for up to 6 weeks. Serve by cutting into very thin slices and serving with cucumber pickle and tomato relish.

Cucumber pickle

Vegetarian

Makes about 5 half-pint (300ml) jars

Ready in 1 hour

2 pounds (900g) unwaxed
  cucumbers, unpeeled and very
  thinly sliced

1 medium red or white onion,
  thinly sliced

1¾ cups (350g) sugar

1 tablespoon salt

1 cup (225ml) cider vinegar or white
  wine vinegar

*Myrtle Allen started making this at Ballymaloe House more than
30 years ago. Not only is it good in burgers and all kinds of
sandwiches, but it's wonderful with cold sliced meats and smoked
fish, and it transforms a humble hard-boiled egg and a chunk of
cheddar into a feast. It's a pickle, so even though it will lose its
vibrant green color, it will keep for up to 3 months.*

*I like to use either a mandoline or a food processor to get very thin
cucumber slices.*

Mix the cucumber and onion in a large bowl. Add the sugar, salt, and
vinegar and mix well to combine. Make 1 hour ahead of when you
want to use it, if possible.

Roast pheasant with wild mushroom, bacon, and thyme stuffing

Serves 3 to 4

Preparation time: 10 minutes

Cooking time: 1½ hours

1 plump young pheasant, plucked and cleaned (or 1 chicken) (2 to 3 pounds/1–1.3kg)

Salt and fresh ground black pepper

3½ tablespoons (40g) butter

FOR THE STUFFING

3½ tablespoons (40g) butter

2⅓ ounces (75g) bacon, cut into cubes (lardons) or dice about ⅜-inch (1cm) in size

½ medium onion, chopped

5 ounces (150g) wild mushrooms, sliced

1 clove garlic, mashed or finely grated

1½ teaspoons fresh thyme, chopped

Salt and freshly ground black pepper

2 cups (100g) fresh bread crumbs

FOR THE GRAVY

1¼ cups (300ml) chicken stock (page 35)

Salt and fresh ground black pepper

Pheasant is a wonderful game bird. It's only available during the winter months' hunting season but it has such a rich, strong flavor that you wouldn't want it year-round. The stuffing uses another autumnal flavor, wild mushrooms. If you can't get wild mushrooms, then you could use button mushrooms, and the flavor will be almost as good.

Serve with Granny's Roasted Herbed Potatoes (page 158), Buttered Cabbage (page 144), Root Vegetable Mash (page 165), and plenty of gravy.

First make the stuffing. Melt half of the butter in a frying pan over medium heat. Add the bacon and cook for 3 to 4 minutes, stirring occasionally, until browned. Add the onion and cook for 5 to 6 minutes, stirring occasionally, until the onion is soft. Next add the mushrooms, garlic, and thyme and season with salt and pepper. Increase the heat to high and cook for about 5 minutes, stirring occasionally, until the mushrooms have softened. Add the remaining butter and, when melted, stir in the bread crumbs until they have soaked up the butter. Allow the stuffing to cool before stuffing the meat.

Preheat the oven to 375°F (190°C/Gas Mark 5).

Put the pheasant in a roasting pan, season the inside and outside with salt and pepper, then fill with the stuffing. Melt the butter in a saucepan over low heat. Add a piece of muslin cloth or cheesecloth to soak, then wrap the pheasant completely in the muslin.

Roast in the oven for 1 to 1¼ hours. Test for doneness by inserting a skewer into the thigh; the juices should run clear and the legs will feel loose. Transfer the pheasant to a carving board, remove the muslin cloth, and allow to rest while you make the gravy.

Place the roasting pan over medium heat and add the chicken stock to deglaze the pan. Bring to a simmer, using a wooden spoon to dislodge and dissolve any caramelized sticky pieces from the bottom of the pan. Taste for seasoning, then pour into a serving pitcher or gravy boat.

Carve the pheasant into slices and serve with the stuffing and gravy.

Vegetables and side dishes

A meal is only as good as its side dishes. A grand roast chicken, for example, should be served with crisp and golden roast potatoes that really do it justice. We Irish are a nation thoroughly in love with the potato, and whether roasted, boiled, mashed, or fried there are few meals served without spuds in this country. It is the baking (floury) varieties that are most popular here—varieties such as Kerr's Pink, Golden Wonder, and Home Guards.

With so many delicious varieties available, vegetables needn't be an afterthought but can be just as delicious and impressive as the meat you serve. Cabbage is a staple of Irish cookery and when cooked gently in butter—not overboiled—it is a seriously special vegetable. Peas and fava (broad) beans make for beautiful and sweet summer treats. Both colcannon (page 170) and champ (page 169) are staples of the Irish table, two divine examples of combining great fresh vegetables with our beloved mashed potatoes.

Lydia's salad with Shanagarry cream dressing

Vegetarian

Serves 2 to 4

Preparation time: 25 minutes

A few handfuls of lettuce leaves

4 tomatoes, quartered

½ cucumber, sliced

4 radishes, sliced

2 small beets, cooked, peeled, and sliced

2 hard-boiled eggs, shelled and quartered

2 scallions

2 tablespoons fresh parsley, chopped

A few sprigs of watercress

FOR THE SHANAGARRY CREAM DRESSING

2 hard-boiled eggs, shelled

1 tablespoon dark brown sugar

Pinch of salt

1 teaspoon dry mustard powder

1 tablespoon malt vinegar

½ cup (125ml) heavy or whipping (double or regular) cream

This salad comes from a Quaker lady, Lydia Strangman, who used to live in Kinoith, the house in which my husband grew up, on the grounds of the Ballymaloe Cookery School. It is wonderfully old-fashioned and salads of the sort would have been served all over the country in days gone by. To my husband Isaac, this is the perfect expression of a salad as comfort food.

The dressing is named after the small village of Shanagarry, which is just next to the Cookery School.

To make the dressing, cut the eggs in half and push the yolks through a sieve and into a bowl. Add the sugar, salt, and mustard powder. Add the vinegar and cream and mix together. Chop the egg whites quite finely and stir half into the dressing mixture; reserve the rest for sprinkling over the salad.

You can arrange the salad on one large plate or on individual serving plates. Arrange the lettuce in the center of the plate, then scatter over the tomatoes, cucumber, radishes, and beets. Arrange the egg quarters on top, then sprinkle over the reserved egg whites, scallions, parsley, and watercress. Drizzle over the dressing and serve immediately.

Munster

Almost two-thirds of Ireland is farmed, and it is lush, green grass that dominates the landscape. Nowhere is the land more rich and fertile on this poetically named Emerald Isle than in the province of Munster. We're a nation of family farmers, and it's in this southerly part of the country that thousands of dairy farmers work the unrivaled land as their ancestors did before them. The farmers of Tipperary, Waterford, and Cork know that grass-fed milk is liquid gold; they own the luxuriant land, the productive cows, and the valuable cooperatives that collect the milk. Between twice-daily milking, thousands of black and white cows graze these green lands, and the dairy produce from this corner of Ireland is exported all over the world. The availability of top-quality grass-fed milk has inspired a plethora of artisans who have brought the ancient tradition of cheese- and yogurt-making to modern Ireland.

Irish farmers have long known that transforming white liquid cream into thick, yellow butter is the best way to preserve this valuable source of fat over the winter months. The tradition of Irish country butter survives and thrives to this day: A gallon of milk is left at room temperature until the thick, delicious cream floats to the surface. This cream is scooped off, churned, separated from the buttermilk (which is used to make soda bread), and washed down with ice-cold water. A slab of butter is a must-have with an Irish dinner, and it's traditionally served in small, rounded balls known as "pats." Homemade country butter had other uses, too. It was thickly smeared over eggs just after they were laid to keep them fresh over the dark winter months when hens stop producing.

Pigs have long had a close affinity with Irish people. The backyard pig was "the gentleman who paid the rent" because it provided much-needed income for tenants. Pigs were slaughtered at home, and no part of the animal was wasted; nothing, that is, apart from the grunt. Bacon was left to hang in the farmhouse chimney where it matured. Bacon and cabbage with parsley sauce is a favorite national dish (see page 144 for a variation). Nutritious fresh pig's blood was a precious resource that was not wasted either, and black pudding was its ideal home. It is fresh blood that gives black pudding its unctuous, silky texture—so good you should eat it with a spoon. Today, the resurgence of interest in fresh blood black pudding has captured the imaginations of butchers such as Jack McCarthy of Kanturk, County Cork, who produces award-winning pudding. Farmers such as Martin and Noreen Conroy of Woodside Farm, Cork, keep alive the tradition of rearing rare breed pigs outdoors, while Frank Murphy operates a small abattoir and butcher shop on Midleton's main street that dates back eight generations. Limerick was known as the "City of Pigs," a nod to the thousands of people who were employed in local bacon factories. The county dish of Limerick is Packet and Tripe. Tripe (the lining of the sheep's stomach) is simmered with onion and milk, with cornstarch added at the end to thicken. It's served piping hot with a portion of freshly congealed pig's blood, the packet.

Beef has always been a prized food, but it is only in recent times that prime cuts of beef have been served on Irish plates. Corned and spiced beef is a Cork specialty (see the recipe on page 132) and, like butter, it was a significant export product during the 17th century. Not for nothing was Cork city referred to as "the slaughterhouse of Ireland." Beef brisket, a cut from the lower chest, is submerged in a brine of water and salt, tied with a cotton string, and boiled with carrots, onions, peppercorns, and mustard for 2 hours. Corned beef is traditionally served with cabbage, potatoes, and mustard.

Salad dressings

Vegetarian

Makes about ⅔ cup (150ml)

Preparation time: 10 minutes

½ cup (100ml) extra virgin olive oil

¼ cup (50ml) freshly squeezed
  lemon juice

Pinch of salt and freshly ground
  black pepper

A great salad is often just as simple as some greens with a dressing, but there are times when you might want to introduce other flavors and textures. Try adding chopped scallions or red onions, diced avocado, olives, toasted pine nuts, or roasted seeds, such as pumpkin, sunflower, or sesame.

To dress the salad, drizzle a little dressing over the dry, washed greens, then toss gently in a bowl. There should be just enough dressing so that the leaves are almost glistening; if they're overdressed, they will be soggy and heavy.

To make the dressing, mix the olive oil and lemon juice in a jar and shake vigorously to combine. Season to taste with salt and pepper. Alternatively, put the ingredients in a bowl and just stir together.

Variations

Honey garlic dressing: To the basic dressing, add 1 peeled and crushed small clove garlic, 1 teaspoon honey, and 1 finely chopped small shallot (or ½ red onion).

Balsamic thyme vinaigrette: Replace the lemon juice with balsamic vinegar and add 1 teaspoon finely chopped thyme leaves to the basic dressing.

Dijon-honey vinaigrette: Replace the lemon juice with cider vinegar and add 1 teaspoon Dijon mustard and 1 teaspoon honey.

Cabbage with bacon and cream

Serves 6 to 8

Preparation time: 10 minutes

Cooking time: 10 minutes

4 tablespoons (50g) butter

6 slices (rashers) of smoked regular (streaky) bacon, thinly sliced

1 large Savoy or green cabbage (about 1⅓ pounds/600g), outer leaves removed

2 cloves garlic, crushed

1 tablespoon water

¾ cup (200ml) light or heavy (single or double) cream

Salt and freshly ground black pepper

This dish turns cabbage into something truly luxurious. The saltiness of the bacon works perfectly with cabbage. It is particularly good served with roast pork or chicken.

Melt the butter in a large frying pan or wok over high heat, add the bacon, and fry for 4 to 5 minutes, until crisp and golden. Remove with a slotted spoon and drain on paper towels.

Meanwhile, cut the cabbage into quarters, removing the core from each piece, and thinly shred across the grain. Add the cabbage to the pan, along with the garlic and water. Sauté for about 5 minutes over medium-high heat, tossing frequently, until wilted and just tender.

Increase the heat a little and return the bacon to the pan. Pour in the cream and allow to bubble for a few minutes until thickened slightly. Season with salt and pepper to taste and serve immediately.

Buttered cabbage

Vegetarian

Serves 4 to 6

Preparation time: 5 minutes

Cooking time: 3 minutes

1 pound (450g) Savoy cabbage (or another dark green, leafy cabbage)

2 tablespoons (25g) butter

2 tablespoons water

Salt and freshly ground black pepper

This is the way we prepare cabbage here at the Ballymaloe Cookery School. The cabbage isn't boiled, but cooked in butter with only a splash of water. This way the water doesn't leech out any flavor or nutrition.

Remove the tough outer leaves from the cabbage. Cut the head of cabbage into four, from top to bottom. Cut out the core, then slice the cabbage crossways into fine shreds, about ¼ inch (5mm) thick.

Combine the butter and water in a wide saucepan over medium heat and allow the butter to melt. Toss in the cabbage and season with salt and pepper. Cover with a lid and cook for 2 to 3 minutes, until just softened; do not let the cabbage burn. Taste immediately for seasoning and serve.

Buttered leeks

Vegetarian

Serves 4 to 6

Preparation time: 5 minutes

Cooking time: 10 minutes

6 medium leeks (about 2 pounds /1kg), washed and dark green tops and roots removed

2 tablespoons (25g) butter

2 tablespoons water

Salt and freshly ground black pepper

2 teaspoons chopped fresh marjoram, chervil, or tarragon (optional)

The leeks are cooked in butter and just a small amount of water, making them richly flavored and wonderfully soft. The most mild of the allium family, leeks are very versatile, and this dish would be just as at home with chicken or pork as with a piece of fish.

Cut the leeks into slices about ¾ inch (2cm) thick.

Combine the butter and water in a saucepan over medium heat. Add the leeks, season with salt and pepper, and stir to mix well. Decrease the heat to very low and cover. If you can, place a disk of waxed paper or butter wrapper on top of the leeks before you add the lid; this keeps them very moist though it isn't essential. Cook for 6 to 10 minutes, until just cooked; the leeks shouldn't lose their fresh green color but should be good and soft. Stir in the chopped herbs (if using), then serve.

Creamed kale

Vegetarian

Serves 4

Preparation time: 5 minutes

Cooking time: 10 minutes

1 pound (450g) curly kale, stems removed (approximately 10 ounces /300g without stems) and finely shredded

½ cup (100ml) light (single) cream

2 tablespoons (25g) butter

Pinch of freshly grated nutmeg

Salt and freshly ground black pepper

Kale is a favorite of mine. and it gets us through the dark winter months when there isn't much green around. This recipe is supremely soothing; the rich cream is offset by just a hint of warming nutmeg. It is a very versatile side dish and works well with roast or grilled meat.

Bring a large saucepan of salted water to a boil over high heat. Add the kale and cook for 3 to 5 minutes, just until tender, then drain the kale and return to the saucepan. Add the cream, butter, and nutmeg and allow to bubble for 2 to 3 minutes, until slightly thickened. Season to taste with salt and pepper and serve while hot.

Pea purée

Vegetarian

Serves 4

Preparation time: 3 minutes

Cooking time: 2 minutes

Salt and freshly ground black
  pepper

1 pound (450g) fresh or frozen peas

6 tablespoons extra virgin olive oil

Good squeeze of lemon juice

Pea purée is naturally sweet and the green color is lovely and intense. Make sure the peas are only just cooked, so they don't lose their bright color and fresh flavor. This purée works especially well with fish, such as mackerel (page 87), but is great served as a dip with tortilla chips.

Bring a saucepan of water to a boil with 1 teaspoon salt. Tip in the peas and cook for 1 to 2 minutes (plus an extra minute for frozen peas), until just soft, then drain well. Combine with the olive oil and blend in a food processor or with a handheld blender until smooth. Add lemon juice and salt and pepper to taste.

Minted fava beans

Vegetarian

Serves 2 to 4

Preparation time: 10 minutes

Cooking time: 5 minutes

Salt and freshly ground black
  pepper

18 ounces (500g) podded fresh or
  frozen fava beans

2 tablespoons (25g) butter

4 tablespoons coarsely chopped
  mint

Fava beans, or broad beans as we call them in Ireland, are one of my favorite summer vegetables. Though a little time-consuming to prepare properly, they are always worth it. The mint here brings its fresh taste, which goes great with the beans, although you can just as easily serve them with parsley or no herbs at all. Keep the leftovers and toss into a salad the next day.

Bring a large saucepan of water to a boil with 1 teaspoon of salt. Add the beans, bring back to a boil, and cook for 2 to 3 minutes if fresh, or 5 to 6 minutes if frozen. Drain well. Once cool enough to handle, pop the beans out of their skins.

Melt the butter in a small saucepan over medium heat. When the butter is frothing, add the beans and toss for 30 to 60 seconds to warm through. Add the mint, tossing it with the beans, and season well with salt and pepper. Spoon into a bowl and serve immediately.

Roast portabello mushrooms with lime cream cheese

Vegetarian

Serves 4

Preparation time: 5 minutes

Cooking time: 15 minutes

8 portabello mushrooms

2 tablespoons extra virgin olive oil

5 tablespoons (25g) finely grated Parmesan cheese

2 cloves garlic, finely chopped

1 teaspoon chopped fresh thyme leaves

Salt and freshly ground black pepper

FOR THE LIME CREAM CHEESE

⅔ cup (150g) cream cheese, softened

1 heaping tablespoon chopped fresh mint

Zest and juice of 1 lime

Juice of ½ lemon

Unsurprisingly, with all our rain and woodlands, we have an abundance of mushrooms every autumn. I love the big flat frills of a portabello mushroom—they look so proud and almost regal. If you can't get portabellos, any big flat mushroom would work well in this recipe.

Preheat the oven to 400°F (200°C/Gas mark 6).

Remove the stems from the portabello mushrooms, arrange the caps on a baking sheet, drizzle with the olive oil, and sprinkle over the Parmesan cheese, garlic, thyme, and some salt and pepper.

Roast for 10 to 15 minutes, until softened. Meanwhile, stir together the cream cheese, mint, lime zest and juice, and lemon juice. Season with salt and pepper to taste.

Spoon the lime cream cheese on top of the mushrooms and serve.

Sticky cumin and apricot roast carrots and parsnips

Vegetarian

Serves 4 to 6

Preparation time: 10 minutes

Cooking time: 45 minutes

18 ounces (500g) small carrots, tops trimmed

18 ounces (500g) small parsnips, peeled and halved (if larger than the carrots)

3 tablespoons extra virgin olive oil

1 teaspoon cumin seeds

Salt and freshly ground black pepper

2 tablespoons apricot jam

2 teaspoons freshly squeezed lemon juice

1 tablespoon chopped fresh cilantro (coriander)

We have great root vegetables and often I cook them simply roasted or in a mash with little dressing up. I do like to get more creative (especially by February when that's all there is growing!), and this dish is a real favorite of mine. The natural sugars in the vegetables work beautifully with the apricot jam.

Preheat the oven to 400°F (200°C /Gas mark 6).

Combine the carrots and parsnips in a large roasting pan and drizzle with the olive oil. Scatter over the cumin seeds, season with salt and pepper, and toss everything together to coat evenly. Roast in the oven for 40 to 45 minutes, tossing occasionally in the oil during cooking, until tender and golden.

In the meantime, heat the apricot jam and lemon juice for a few minutes in a small saucepan, stirring until you have a smooth, runny sauce. Pour this over the carrots and parsnips for the last 10 minutes of cooking, tossing the vegetables in the sauce to coat evenly. Sprinkle with the cilantro just before serving.

Cauliflower cheese

Vegetarian

Serves 4 to 6

Preparation time: 5 minutes

Cooking time: 15 minutes

Salt and freshly ground black pepper

1 cauliflower, broken into small to medium florets, leaves reserved

1¼ cups (300ml) Basic White Sauce (page 114) made with 3 tablespoons all-purpose (plain) flour and 3 tablespoons butter

¼ teaspoon dry mustard powder

⅔ cup (75g) grated cheese (cheddar, Gruyère, Stilton, whatever you have!)

Good pinch of nutmeg (freshly grated, if possible)

1 tablespoon chopped fresh parsley

Cauliflower cheese is maybe the most nostalgic dish to me. My mum would often make it when I was young. She'd mostly use whatever cheese was in the fridge, but usually a creamy cheese like a cheddar. This is supremely comforting food to serve with roast chicken (see page 96) or beef.

Fill a large saucepan with about 1 inch (3cm) water and add a little salt. Arrange the cauliflower leaves in the bottom, sit the cauliflower florets on top, cover with a lid, and bring to a boil. Cook for 8 to 10 minutes, until the stems are tender when pierced with a knife. Remove the cauliflower (discarding the leaves), drain well, and arrange in a single layer in a large gratin dish.

In the meantime, make the cheese sauce. Start with the white sauce in a small saucepan over low heat and add the mustard and most of the grated cheese, reserving a little to scatter over the top of the dish, and stir until melted. Season to taste with salt, pepper, and nutmeg.

Preheat the broiler (grill) to high. Pour the sauce over the cauliflower in the dish and then scatter the reserved cheese on top. Broil (grill) for 2 to 3 minutes, until golden and bubbling on top. Scatter the chopped parsley over and serve.

Rachel's tip
Once the cauliflower cheese is assembled in the dish, it can be popped in the fridge for a few hours until you are ready to serve. Before broiling (grilling), reheat the cauliflower cheese in a preheated 400°F (200°C /Gas mark 6) oven for about 20 minutes.

Granny's roasted herbed potatoes

Vegetarian (if made with olive oil)

Serves 4 to 6

Preparation time: 10 minutes

Cooking time: 1 hour

8 to 10 large baking or russet (floury) potatoes, peeled and, if large, cut in half

Olive oil, duck or goose fat, or beef dripping

Salt

4 sprigs of fresh thyme, or 2 sprigs of rosemary

Some roast meats, like lamb or traditional stuffed chicken, simply demand really good roasted potatoes as an accompaniment. My late grandmother used to make the best roasted potatoes, the ones that are crispy and crunchy on the outside, and soft on the inside. The trick is to parboil the potatoes, then drain them and shake them in the saucepan before roasting.

Preheat the oven to 425°F (220°C/Gas mark 7).

Drop the potatoes into boiling salted water and cook for 10 minutes. Drain off the water and shake the potatoes around in the dry saucepan with the lid on—this roughens the surface of the potatoes and makes them cook up crispier.

Heat a few tablespoons of olive oil in a roasting pan on top of the stove, add the potatoes and toss, making sure the potatoes are well coated (add more fat if they are not). Sprinkle with salt and roast in the hot oven for 35 to 55 minutes, basting (spooning the hot oil or fat over them) every now and then and turning over after 20 minutes or so. When they are nearly cooked, tuck the herb sprigs in between the potatoes. You can turn the oven down to 400°F (200°C/Gas mark 6) after 15 to 20 minutes if you think they are dark enough. If the potatoes have to keep warm in the oven for any amount of time, do not cover them or they will go soggy.

Traditional herb stuffing

Makes about 3 cups (250g)

Preparation time: 5 minutes

Cooking time: 10 minutes

2 tablespoons (25g) butter

1 tablespoon extra virgin olive oil

1 onion, chopped

1 clove garlic, finely chopped

3 tablespoons chopped mixed fresh herbs, such as parsley, thyme, and sage

2 cups (100g) fresh white bread crumbs

Salt and freshly ground black pepper

Stuffing may have once been used to bulk out more expensive meat, but it is cooked now as a delicious dish in its own right, and many people in Ireland would revolt if they were served a roast bird without stuffing. This is a great basic stuffing recipe with lots of variations for you to try. Do experiment with your own favorite herbs and ingredients. This stuffing can be made in advance and kept in the fridge for a couple of days or frozen.

Combine the butter and olive oil in a saucepan over low heat. Add the onion and garlic, cover with a butter wrapper or a piece of waxed (greaseproof) paper, and then cover with a lid. Cook for 8 to 10 minutes, until the onions are soft but not browned. Take off the heat, remove the lid and paper cover, and stir in the herbs and bread crumbs. Season to taste with salt and pepper.

Variations

Lemony stuffing: (Makes about 3 cups/250g)
Stir the finely grated zest of 1 lemon and the juice of ½ lemon into the stuffing mixture at the same time as the herbs and bread crumbs (see above).

Chorizo stuffing: (Makes about 4 cups/350g)
Cook 4 ounces (110g) very finely chopped dried chorizo sausage with the onion. Basil, thyme, and marjoram would go well with this as the mixed herbs.

Smoked bacon stuffing: (Makes about 3½ cups/325g)
Use a red onion in place of a yellow one, and cook with 2 ounces (50g) chopped smoked bacon or pancetta. Use thyme and/or parsley as the herbs.

Ivan Whelan's chestnut stuffing: (Makes about 5 cups/450g)
Stir 5 ounces (150g) finely chopped and toasted chestnuts into the stuffing mixture. Use sage and/or rosemary as the herbs. For Christmas stuffing, add 6 tablespoons (50g) dried cranberries as well.

Fruit and nut stuffing: (Makes about 5 cups/450g)
This variation goes surprisingly well with chicken. Stir ⅓ cup (50g) chopped dried apricots, ⅓ cup (50g) golden raisins (sultanas), and ⅓ cup (50g) chopped and toasted hazelnuts into the stuffing mixture.

Sautéed potatoes with caramelized onions

Vegetarian

Serves 4

Preparation time: 10 minutes

Cooking time: 40 minutes

1½ pounds (800g) russet or baking (floury) potatoes, peeled and cut into ¾-inch (2cm) cubes

4 tablespoons extra virgin olive oil

Salt and freshly ground black pepper

2 tablespoons (25g) butter

1 large onion, thinly sliced

2 cloves garlic, finely chopped

2 teaspoons finely chopped fresh thyme or rosemary leaves

What I love about this recipe is that two humble ingredients are brought together, and with just a little effort they're made into something really special. The onions become golden and sweet in the pan, while the potatoes are crispy on the outside but wonderfully fluffy on the inside. This is delicious with any roast meat, a steak, or even a burger. Use any leftover mixture in a frittata or omelet. You can omit the onions and just serve the sautéed potatoes, if you desire.

Dry the potatoes well in a clean kitchen towel. Pour 3 tablespoons of the olive oil into a large, heavy frying pan over high heat and add the potatoes. Turn the heat down to low to medium and sauté the potatoes for 30 to 35 minutes, tossing regularly, until softened, crisp, and golden. Season well with salt and pepper.

In the meantime, heat the butter and remaining 1 tablespoon oil in a separate frying pan over low to medium heat. When the butter has melted, add the onion. Cook for about the same length of time, 30 to 35 minutes, until softened and caramelized to a golden color. Add the garlic and thyme to the onions during the last 5 minutes of cooking and season well with salt and pepper.

Tip the caramelized onions into the pan with the sautéed potatoes, toss together, and serve immediately.

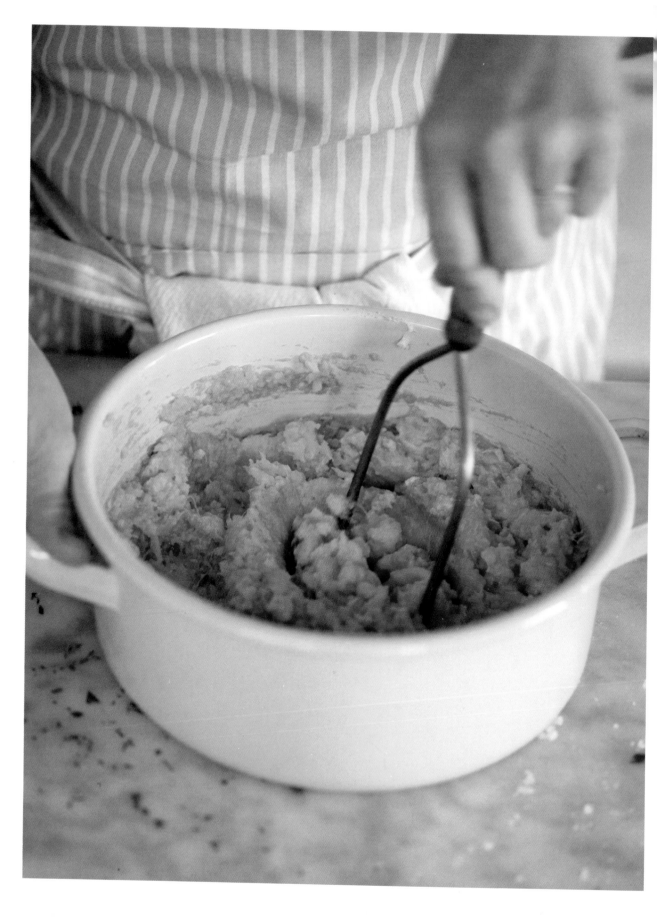

Root vegetable mash

Vegetarian

Serves 4 to 6

Preparation time: 15 minutes

Cooking time: 20 to 25 minutes

1 carrot, cut into ¾-inch (2cm) chunks

Salt and freshly ground black pepper

1 parsnip, peeled and cut into ¾-inch (2cm) chunks

½ celery root (celeriac), peeled and cut into ¾-inch (2cm) chunks

1 sweet new potato, peeled and cut into ¾-inch (2cm) chunks

2 tablespoons butter or olive oil

2 tablespoons heavy or whipping (double or regular) cream (optional)

1 tablespoon chopped fresh parsley

1 tablespoon chopped fresh thyme or rosemary leaves

For a variation on standard mashed potato, why not try making it with other root vegetables? This recipe uses a mixture of parsnip, celery root, and sweet potato for a luxurious mash that's full of flavor. What's great about this side dish is that it works well with whatever root vegetables you have. This recipe should be considered a guideline only; try using more or less of any of the vegetables, or you could add Jerusalem artichokes, turnips, or even beets. With butter and cream, you can turn modest ingredients into something quite luxurious.

Put the carrot in a large saucepan and cover with cold water, adding a good pinch of salt. Bring to a boil, then decrease the heat to medium-high and simmer for 5 minutes. Tip in the parsnip, celery root, and sweet potato and continue cooking for another 15 minutes, or until all the vegetables are tender.

Drain well, then add the butter and the cream (if using). Mash the vegetables either by hand or in a food processor for a smoother purée. Taste for seasoning, adding pepper and more salt if needed, then stir in the chopped herbs and serve.

Creamy mashed potato

Vegetarian

Serves 4

Preparation time: 10 minutes

Cooking time: 30 minutes

2¼ pounds (1kg) baking or russet (floury) potatoes, scrubbed clean

Salt and freshly ground black pepper

4 tablespoons (50g) butter

¾ cup (200ml) milk, or ½ cup (150ml) milk and ¼ cup (50ml) light or heavy (single or double) cream, plus more if needed

Good mashed potato is the best comfort food ever, eaten on its own with a great pat of butter melting in it. It is hugely popular in our family—we'd eat it for every meal! For the most nutritious version—and the fluffiest mash—boil the potatoes in their skins and peel afterwards. Baking or russet (floury) potatoes are always best as new potatoes are too waxy for mashing.

Put the potatoes in a large saucepan, cover with cold water, and add a good pinch of salt. Bring the water to a boil and cook the potatoes for 10 minutes. Then pour out all but about 1½ inches (4cm) of the water, cover, and continue to cook the potatoes over very low heat. Don't be tempted to stick a knife into them at any stage to see if they are cooked—the skins will split and the potatoes will just break up and become soggy if you do. About 20 minutes later, when you think the potatoes might be cooked, test them with a skewer; if they are soft, take them off the heat and drain them.

Peel the potatoes while they are still hot, holding them in a clean kitchen towel to avoid scalding your hands. Mash them immediately. Add the butter, but don't add any milk until the potatoes are free of lumps. Bring the milk to a boil in a small saucepan. Slowly stir the boiling milk into the potatoes—you may not need it all, or you may need more, depending on the texture of the potatoes. Season to taste with salt and pepper.

Rachel's tip

If you want to make the mash in advance, add a little extra milk, to keep the potatoes moist as they sit. The mash keeps well in a warm oven as long as it is covered with a lid, plate, or aluminum foil.

Boxty

Vegetarian

Serves 4

Preparation time: 5 minutes

Cooking time: 20 minutes

1 egg

¼ cup (50ml) light (single) cream

9 ounces (250g) baking or russet (floury) potatoes, peeled and coarsely grated

2 tablespoons (15g) all-purpose (plain) flour

Salt and freshly ground black pepper

2 tablespoons (25g) butter

Boxty are traditional potato pancakes that are particularly loved in the Northern counties. They can be served as a potato side dish rather than mashed or boiled potatoes or as part of an Irish breakfast (page 108). This is my husband Isaac's take on boxty, he uses cream and not too much flour so they're good and rich.

In a bowl, whisk together the egg with the cream. Add the potato and flour, season with salt and pepper, and stir to mix. The mixture will be slightly runny.

Melt the butter in a frying pan over medium heat. Add the potato mixture and cook for 8 to 10 minutes on each side, until the surface is golden brown and the potato is cooked through. Remove to a serving plate and cut into wedges to serve.

Pea and scallion champ

Vegetarian

Serves 6 to 8

Preparation time: 10 minutes

Cooking time: 40 minutes

3⅓ pounds (1.5kg) baking or russet (floury) potatoes, scrubbed clean

Salt and freshly ground black pepper

7 tablespoons (100g) butter

2 cups (500ml) milk or 1⅔ cups (400ml) milk and ⅓ cup (100ml) light (single) cream

1 pound (450g) fresh or frozen peas

¾ cup (75g) sliced scallions (spring onions)

4 tablespoons chopped fresh parsley

Champ is a dish made throughout Ireland, similar to colcannon, but made with scallions. I've added peas for their sweetness and to make this dish a little more substantial. The peas and scallions are cooked in the milk so their flavor infuses the whole dish. This champ makes a versatile side dish and goes well with any meat, especially bacon or pork.

Fill a large saucepan with water, then add the potatoes and a good pinch of salt. Bring to a boil and boil for 10 minutes. Then pour all but about 1½ inches (4cm) of the water out of the pan, cover, and continue to cook the potatoes over very low heat. (Don't be tempted to stick a knife into them as the skins will break and they will disintegrate.) Continue to cook for another 20 to 30 minutes, until a skewer goes in easily.

Drain the potatoes, peel while they are still hot, and put into a bowl along with three-quarters of the butter. Mash immediately by hand, or beat in an electric stand mixer fitted with the paddle attachment, until they are free of lumps.

Bring the milk (or milk and cream) to a boil in a small saucepan. Add the peas and scallions and boil for 2 minutes. Then add the parsley and remove from the heat. Add most of this mixture to the potatoes, season with salt and pepper, and beat until creamy and smooth. Add more of the milk mixture if necessary (you might not need all of it, but do add in all of the peas and scallions using a slotted spoon), then serve hot with the remaining butter melting in the center.

Roast garlic colcannon

Vegetarian

Serves 4 to 6

Preparation time: 15 minutes

Cooking time: 1¼ hours

1 large bulb garlic, left whole and unpeeled

2 tablespoons extra virgin olive oil

Salt and ground black pepper

1 sprig of rosemary

2¼ pounds (1kg) baking or russet (floury) potatoes, scrubbed clean

1 pound (450g) Savoy cabbage or kale

1 cup (250ml) milk

4 tablespoons (50g) butter, plus extra to serve

Colcannon is a traditional Irish dish made from mashed potato and cabbage or kale. By roasting the garlic, its flesh is tempered and tamed to become sweet and mellow.

Preheat the oven to 425°F (220°C/Gas mark 7).

Place the whole bulb of garlic in a small ovenproof dish, drizzle with the olive oil, season with salt and pepper, and add the sprig of rosemary. Cover with aluminum foil and roast for about 45 minutes, until the garlic has completely softened.

Put the potatoes in a large saucepan and cover with cold water. Add a good pinch of salt, cover with a lid, and bring to a boil. After 10 minutes, strain off two-thirds of the water, put the lid back on the pan, and cook over gentle heat so that the potatoes steam for about 30 minutes, until they are tender.

Remove and discard the dark tough outer leaves from the cabbage (if using). Wash the rest and cut into quarters, removing the core. Cut the cabbage across the grain into slices about ¼ inch (5mm) thick. Place in another large saucepan, add the milk, and simmer for about 4 minutes or until tender. If you're using kale, cut out the tough center rib of the leaves, then slice and cook in milk as for the cabbage.

When the potatoes are just cooked, peel them while still warm and immediately mash them with the butter and some salt and pepper. Use your fingers to squeeze out the roasted garlic pulp and beat into the potatoes with enough boiling milk from the cabbage to make a fluffy purée. Then drain the cooked cabbage or kale, stir into the mash, and taste for seasoning.

For perfection, serve immediately in a hot dish with a lump of butter melting on top.

Desserts and cakes

A truly delicious dessert can really make a meal. Since I was a young girl I have always enjoyed making desserts. I do have a real sweet tooth and, even if it's just a morsel, I crave a little something sweet after my meal.

The desserts in Ireland often feature the fruits we can grow here, which means tarts and crumbles packed full of our gorgeous apples, pears, and lots of lovely berries. There are also more specifically Irish dishes such as Carrageen Moss Pudding (page 197) (which uses a type of seaweed). This chapter also includes a few recipes that use the delicious flavors of Irish coffee, and there's also a recipe for the drink itself (page 210).

Darina's summer pudding

Vegetarian	
Serves 12 to 16	
Preparation time: 30 minutes	
Cooking time: 30 minutes	
Ready in 8 hours	

2 (7-inch/18cm) sponge cakes
(see page 176)

2¾ cups (550g) granulated or
superfine (caster) sugar

3¼ cups (725ml) water

2 cups (225g) black currants,
fresh or frozen

2 cups (225g) red currants, fresh
or frozen

2 cups (225g) raspberries, fresh
or frozen

2 cups (225g) strawberries, fresh
or frozen

Vanilla ice cream or softly whipped
cream, to serve

This is my mother-in-law Darina's recipe, which we teach in the cookery school. It's such a celebration of summer berries, their flavors mixing and melding together as the pudding sets in the fridge. This summer pudding uses cake rather than bread to line the bowl. That extra dimension of sweetness makes it really special, and it should be served with lots of softly whipped cream.

Make sure the fruit and syrup is boiling when you pour it into the cake-lined bowl, otherwise the syrup won't properly soak in. You can use either fresh or frozen berries.

Cut each round of sponge cake in half, horizontally. Set aside one of the halves for topping the pudding.

Line a large bowl with cake in a single layer. A plastic bowl is useful because it can be squeezed to make unmolding easier, but it's not essential; use whatever large bowl you have. The softer side of the cake should be against the bowl. You will need to cut the cake halves into a few pieces to make a sort of patchwork of cake with which to line the bowl. I try and use a few large pieces to begin with then make up the lining by cutting smaller pieces from the remaining cake halves. When you are done, the bowl should be lined with a single layer of cake going all the way up the sides but you will have some scraps left over. Reserve these scraps for later, along with the reserved cake half. Place the cake-lined bowl in a gratin or baking dish.

Combine the sugar and water in a saucepan over medium heat, stirring to dissolve the sugar, and bring to a boil. Boil for 2 minutes, then add the black currants and red currants and cook until the fruit bursts, 3 to 4 minutes. Stir in the raspberries and strawberries and remove from the heat.

Ladle some of the hot syrup and fruit into the sponge cake-lined bowl. When about half full, add the remaining scraps of cake, then fill right up to the top of the bowl with the rest of the fruit (using a slotted spoon) and some more of the syrup. Reserve any excess syrup and place in the fridge. Cover the pudding with the reserved cake half, making a lid for it all, the juice may overflow a little (that's what the gratin or baking dish is for). Put a plate right side up on top

recipe continues overleaf

and press down with a heavy weight (such as two cans of tomatoes or beans); more juice will overflow. Allow to cool, then place in the fridge for at least 8 hours or overnight (but it will keep for 3 to 4 days).

To serve, turn the pudding upside down onto a deep serving dish, unmold by gently squeezing the bowl to free the pudding, then lift the bowl off. Pour any leftover syrup over the top. Serve with vanilla ice cream or softly whipped cream.

Sponge cake

Vegetarian

Makes 2 (7-inch/18cm) layers

Preparation time: 15 minutes

Cooking time: 25 minutes

½ cup (125g) butter, softened

14 tablespoons (175g) superfine (caster) sugar

3 eggs

1½ cups plus 1 tablespoon (175g) all-purpose (plain) flour

1 teaspoon baking powder

1 tablespoon milk

Preheat the oven to 350°F (180°C/Gas Mark 4).

Use a little butter to grease two (7-inch/18cm) cake pans, then sprinkle with a little flour and line the bottom of each with a round of parchment paper.

In a bowl, using a wooden spoon, or an electric mixer with a paddle attachment, cream the butter. Gradually add the sugar, beating until soft and light and quite pale in color. Add the eggs, one at a time, and beat well between each addition. Sift in the flour and baking powder, then mix everything together lightly and add the milk to moisten. Divide the mixture evenly between the two cake pans and make a little dip in the center of each to ensure an even rise.

Bake for 20 to 25 minutes, until a skewer inserted into the middle comes out clean. Place on a wire rack to cool.

Fluffy lemon pudding

Vegetarian

Serves 6

Preparation time: 15 minutes

Cooking time: 40 minutes

4 tablespoons (50g) butter, softened

1¼ cups (250g) superfine (caster) or
  granulated sugar

3 eggs, separated

9½ tablespoons (75g) all-purpose
  (plain) flour

1¼ cups (300ml) milk

Finely grated zest and juice of
  2 lemons

Confectioners' (icing) sugar,
  for dusting

*When cooked, this delectable pudding has a layer of lemon sponge
sitting on top of a pool of hot lemon curd. This has been made at
Ballymaloe for years because it is a favorite of so many people.*

Preheat the oven to 350°F (180°C/Gas mark 4).

Beat the butter by hand in a large bowl or with a stand mixer fitted
with the paddle attachment until it is really soft and creamy. Add the
sugar and beat until pale and fluffy. Add the egg yolks, one at a time,
beating each one in before adding the next. Sift in the flour and add
the milk and lemon zest and juice, and mix well together.

Whisk the egg whites in a large, spotlessly clean bowl until they
form stiff peaks. Gently fold the egg whites into the cake mixture
until well mixed. Pour the mixture into a 5-cup (1.2l) oval pie dish
(7 by 9 inches/18 by 23cm) with 2-inch (5cm) sides.

Bake for 30 to 40 minutes, until golden and set on top, but not set
underneath. Remove from the oven and allow to cool slightly before
sprinkling with confectioners' sugar and serving.

Variation

Individual puddings: Use six small to medium ramekins or ovenproof
cups arranged on a baking sheet and bake for 15 to 20 minutes, or
until just set. Serve as above.

Fruit pies

Vegetarian

Serves 8 to 10

Preparation time: 30 minutes

Cooking time: 50 minutes

Ready in 1½ hours

¾ cup (175g) butter, softened

4 tablespoons (50g) superfine
(caster) or granulated sugar, plus
extra for sprinkling

2 eggs

2 cups (250g) all-purpose (plain)
flour, plus extra for dusting

Fruit filling (see page 182)

Softly whipped cream or custard

A seasonal fruit pie is one of the mainstays of Irish desserts. It could be filled with apples and blackberries in the autumn, gooseberries in the summer, or rhubarb in the spring. Many Irish farmhouses grow fruit, and it always find its way into a tart of this sort. The pastry isn't fancy, just a simple but delicious buttery pastry, similar to one that Mrs. O'Connell, my husband's late grandmother, used to make.

My mother-in-law always insists on serving desserts like this with softly whipped cream and with a good sprinkling of brown sugar. It's really worth doing; the cream accentuates the sweetness of the pie, a little like sprinkling salt over a savory dish.

To make the pastry, use a handheld beater or an electric stand mixer fitted with a dough hook and cream the butter and sugar together until pale and creamy. Add one egg, beating continuously. Beat the second egg in a separate bowl. Pour half of it into the mixture (reserving the remainder for later) and beat again. Sift over the flour and stir in gently to make a smooth, soft dough. Tip the dough onto a clean work surface and knead a little before dividing in two. Shape each piece into a flat round, cover with plastic wrap (cling film), and leave in the fridge for at least 1 hour.

Preheat the oven to 350°F (180°C/Gas mark 4). Lightly butter a 9-inch (23cm) pie pan or tart pan.

Place each pastry half on a floured work surface and roll out to a thickness of about ⅛ inch (3mm). Use one piece to line the pan, trimming off the excess pastry with the back of a knife. Brush a little of the reserved beaten egg around the edge of the pastry.

Add your chosen fruit filling (see overleaf) to the pastry and top with the second rolled-out piece of pastry, trimming the excess once again and pressing the edges together to seal. Use any leftover pastry to decorate the top by rolling it out and cutting it into shapes. Brush all over with the remaining beaten egg.

Bake for 45 to 50 minutes, until the fruit is tender when tested with a skewer and the pastry is golden. Remove from the oven, lightly sprinkle with sugar, and allow to cool slightly. Cut into wedges and serve with whipped cream or custard.

recipe continues overleaf

Fruit fillings

Apple: Peel, core, and dice 1½ pounds (700g) Bramley or other cooking apples and toss with ¾ cup (150g) granulated sugar and 2 to 3 cloves.

Plum, nectarine, or peach: Halve, pit, and quarter 2 pounds (900g) plums, nectarines, or peeled peaches and toss with 6 tablespoons (75g) superfine (caster) or granulated sugar and 2 tablespoons cornstarch (cornflour). Add an additional teaspoon of the cornstarch if the fruit is very ripe.

Strawberry: Toss 1½ pounds (700g) hulled strawberries (halved if large) with 1 tablespoon cornstarch (cornflour) and 4 tablespoons (50g) superfine (caster) or granulated sugar.

Custard

Vegetarian

Makes 3 cups (700 ml)

Preparation time: 5 minutes

Cooking time: 15 minutes

2 cups (500ml) milk

5 egg yolks

½ cup (100g) superfine (caster) sugar

Custard is the perfect accompaniment for a fruit pie or crumble (pages 180 and 190). This recipe takes me right back to my childhood.

Pour the milk into a large saucepan and slowly bring to a boil. Meanwhile, beat the egg yolks and sugar together in a large bowl until pale and thick. Gradually whisk the hot milk into the beaten eggs and sugar and pour the whole mixture back into the saucepan.

Return to low heat and cook gently for 5 to 8 minutes, stirring all the time, until the custard thickens slightly (it should just coat the back of the spoon). Pour into a warm pitcher to serve. If reheating, do so very gently over low heat so that the eggs don't scramble.

Variations

Vanilla custard: Add 1 vanilla bean, split, to the milk when bringing to a boil in the pan. Remove the bean from the custard before pouring it into the pitcher to serve. Yummy with plum or rhubarb crumble (page 192).

Orange custard: Add 1 strip of orange zest to the milk when bringing to a boil in the pan. Remove the zest from the custard before pouring it into the pitcher to serve. Goes especially well with the Steamed Ginger Treacle Pudding (page 214).

Irish apple cake

Vegetarian
Serves 4 to 6
Preparation time: 30 minutes
Cooking time: 50 minutes
Ready in 1½ hours

1¾ cups (225g) all-purpose (plain) flour

½ teaspoon baking powder

½ cup (100g) butter

½ cup (100g) sugar, plus 2 tablespoons

1 egg, beaten

Approximately ½ cup (100ml) milk

1 large cooking apple, about 10½ ounces (300g) in weight

1 teaspoon ground cinnamon

Softly whipped cream, to serve

This wonderful cake is a delicious way to make the most of the autumn apples. My husband's grandmother, Myrtle Allen, has been making this for many years, and it is still made today at Ballymaloe.

Preheat the oven to 350°F (180°C/Gas Mark 4). Butter a 10-inch (25cm) pie pan.

Mix the flour with the baking powder. Rub in the butter with your fingertips until the texture resembles bread crumbs. Add the ½ cup sugar, beaten egg, and enough milk to form a soft dough. Pat out half of the dough in the greased pie pan (don't worry—it is supposed to be very wet).

Peel, core, and chop the apple into ¾-inch (2cm) cubes. Arrange the apples on the dough and sprinkle with 1 tablespoon sugar and the cinnamon. Gently spoon out the remaining dough on top of the apples to cover them completely. Sprinkle with the remaining 1 tablespoon sugar and cut a slit through the middle of the top dough.

Bake for 40 to 50 minutes, until golden and crunchy on the outside (the apples should be soft on the inside). Serve with softly whipped cream.

Rachel's tip
If the butter is cold (just taken from the fridge), grate it into the flour and it will rub in within a couple of seconds.

Connacht

Connacht is renowned for its dramatic, cloud-capped mountains and glacial lakes, its wet bog land and indented coastline. Small villages pepper the region and it is here, in the public houses, that farmers and fishermen gather with the locals over a pint. Depending on the vagaries of the weather, the mighty Atlantic Ocean gently soothes or vigorously batters the majestic western coast of this captivating province, which encompasses Galway, Mayo, Sligo, Leitrim, and Roscommon.

Overlooking the wild Atlantic seas in North Mayo is the Céide Fields. It was here, nearly 6,000 years ago, that Stone Age communities produced food from the land. In the 1930s, vestiges of ancient field systems were discovered beneath a blanket of peat, along with evidence of dwellings and cultivated fields of wheat and barley. The skills from these early Mayo farmers have been handed down through the generations, and farmers across these scenic counties continue to work the land today.

The abundant rain, aided by the warm Gulf Stream, creates the optimum climate for grass to grow in these wet, warm, western fields. Unsurprisingly, cattle favor this nutritious and bountiful food. Cows have pervaded the Irish psyche for centuries—the Irish for road, bóthar, translates as "cow-track" and an 8th-century Irish text boasts of high-quality marbled meat from cattle fed nothing but "full new milk and liugfér" (newly mown grass) as calves. Today, the offspring of spring-calving cows suckle their mothers' milk for nine months before weaning to grass. Suckler herds of Angus, Hereford, Limousin, Charolais, Simmental, and Belgian Blue breeds produce world-class Irish beef. Native Irish rare breeds such as Dexter, Irish Moiled, and Droimeann cattle can be seen grazing the stone-walled fields of Connacht, too.

The rocky, rough uplands are more suited to hardy sheep such as the Blackface mountain breed, which dates back to the 1800s. The moist Atlantic sea spray finds its way to the Connemara fields where these sheep graze, and this salty mist enhances the growth of the wild grasses, heathers, herbs, and flowers. The result is Connemara Hill lamb, a meat that is imbued with sweet and salty flavors and is considered so unique that a sought-after stamp from European authorities ensures that only lamb produced on these majestic mountains can be labeled as "Connemara Hill lamb." For many people, it is lamb that is the core ingredient in Irish stew (see the recipe on page 80), and you will not find a finer-tasting meat than young sheep reared on the sweet grasses of the Connemara hills.

The revered Atlantic salmon is enshrined in Irish mythology and folklore, and also in the history of Irish food. Fishermen and locals await late autumn with excitement and anticipation, for this is the time of the salmon run. Hordes of agile salmon return from the salty ocean and enter their natal freshwater rivers to spawn. In the 1700s, salmon was roasted over the rising smoke of the turf fire; in recent history, a whole salmon was seasoned and then tightly wrapped in sheets of yesterday's newspaper and cooked over an open fire. Today, artisans such as the Roberts family, who own and run the oldest smokehouse in Connemara, ensure that the tradition of hand-filleting and hand-smoking salmon continues.

Sweet scones with blueberry jam

Vegetarian

Makes 10 scones and 2 half-pint (300ml) jars of jam

Preparation time: 40 minutes

Cooking time: 30 minutes

Ready in 45 minutes

3½ cups (450g) all-purpose (plain) flour

Pinch of salt

4¼ teaspoons (20g) baking powder

2 tablespoons (25g) superfine (caster) or granulated sugar

6 tablespoons (75g) butter, softened

2 eggs

¾ cup (200ml) milk

FOR THE JAM
3¾ cups (375g) blueberries, fresh or frozen

2 tablespoons water

1½ cups (300g) sugar

3 tablespoons freshly squeezed lemon juice

FOR A CRUNCHY GLAZE (OPTIONAL)
1 small egg, beaten (if there is no liquid left from the scones)

Granulated sugar

Butter, whipped cream, or clotted cream, to serve

Afternoon tea just wouldn't be right without scones! They are so simple and delicious, particularly with homemade jam, which is much easier to make than many people realize. This scone recipe comes from Elizabeth O'Connell, Isaac's maternal grandmother.

First make the jam, which will then keep in a cool place for several months. Place a saucer in the fridge for testing the jam later. To sterilize the jars (any shape will do, preferably with a lid), put them through a dishwasher cycle, boil in a pan of water for 5 minutes, or place in a preheated oven (300°F/150°C/Gas mark 2) for 10 minutes.

Combine the blueberries and water in a saucepan over medium heat. Bring to a boil and mash the fruit with a potato masher. Add the sugar and lemon juice and stir over high heat for 5 minutes. Test by placing a small blob on the chilled saucer, leave for 20 seconds, and run your finger through the blob. If it forms a skin, the jam is set. Carefully remove the jars from the dishwasher, pan, or oven, using oven mitts, if necessary. Pour the jam into the jars immediately and cover with their lids and screwbands.

To make the scones, preheat the oven to 450°F (230°C/Gas mark 8). Lightly flour a baking sheet.

Sift the flour, salt, and baking powder into a large bowl; add the sugar and mix. Rub in the butter and make a well in the center. In another bowl, whisk the eggs and then add the milk. Pour all but ¼ cup (60ml) of this liquid into the dry ingredients and, using one hand, mix to a soft dough, adding more of the liquid, if necessary.

Turn out onto a floured work surface and knead until a dough is formed. Sprinkle with flour and gently roll out until it is ¾ to 2 inches (2–5cm) thick. Cut with a knife or a round 2-inch (5cm) cutter into scones. Place on the prepared baking sheet.

If you opt for a crunchy glaze, brush the scones with the liquid left in the bowl or with a beaten egg, then dip each one, wet side down, into the granulated sugar. Return to the baking sheet, sugared side up.

Bake in the center of the oven for 7 to 10 minutes, until golden brown on top. Cool on a wire rack. Serve split with butter and jam or with jam and a blob of whipped cream or clotted cream.

Fruit crumbles

Vegetarian

Serves 6

Preparation time: 15 minutes

Cooking time: 40 minutes

Ready in 2 hours

Fruit filling (see below and overleaf)

6 tablespoons (75g) butter, diced

1¼ cups (150g) all-purpose (plain)
flour

⅓ cup (75g) packed light brown
sugar

Confectioners' (icing) sugar, for
dusting

Lightly whipped cream, ice cream,
or custard (page 182), to serve

*A fruit crumble is a divine yet simple dessert. It's one of the first
dessert recipes we teach here at the Ballymaloe Cookery School.
Once you know the technique for making the topping, you can use
it to cover whatever fruit you have on hand. I love to serve this dish
with flavored homemade custard (page 182).*

Preheat the oven to 350°F (180°C/Gas mark 4). Lightly butter a 5-cup
(1l) oval (6 by 8-inch/15 by 20cm) baking dish with 2 inch (5cm) sides
or six individual ½-cup (120ml) ramekins. Set on a baking sheet.

Prepare your choice of fruit filling from the following list and spread
evenly in the bottom of the baking dish or ramekins.

To make the crumble topping, rub the flour and butter together in a
large bowl until it resembles very coarse bread crumbs (don't rub it in
too much or the crumble won't be crunchy once cooked). Stir in the
sugar. Sprinkle the topping over the fruit. (At this point you can place
the crumble in the fridge for up to 48 hours or freeze until you want
to bake it.)

Bake the crumble for 35 to 40 minutes in a baking dish (15 to 20
minutes in the ramekins), until golden and bubbly. Serve dusted with
confectioners' sugar and with a dollop of lightly whipped cream.

Fruit fillings

Apple and raspberry: Cook 1⅓ pounds (600g) (about 2) peeled, cored,
and coarsely chopped cooking apples (such as Bramley or Granny
Smith) with 4 tablespoons (50g) superfine (caster) or granulated sugar
and 1 tablespoon of water for 6 to 8 minutes, until soft. Spoon into
the prepared baking dish and sprinkle over 1⅔ cups (200g) fresh or
frozen raspberries.

Apple and sweet mincemeat: Cook 3 to 4 (1¾ pounds/800g) peeled,
cored, and coarsely chopped cooking apples (such as Bramley
or Granny Smith) with 6 tablespoons (75g) superfine (caster) or
granulated sugar and 2 tablespoons of water for 6 to 8 minutes, or
until just softened. Toss with ½ cup (4 ounces/110g) sweet mincemeat
pie filling (mince pie filling) and spoon into the prepared baking dish.

recipe continues overleaf

Strawberry and rhubarb: Cook 1 pound (450g) rhubarb, coarsely chopped, with 6 tablespoons (75g) sugar and 1 tablespoon of water for about 5 minutes, until it begins to soften. Spoon into the prepared baking dish and sprinkle over 1⅓ cups (225g) hulled and quartered strawberries.

Plum and vanilla: Dissolve 6 tablespoons (75g) superfine (caster) or granulated sugar in ½ cup (100ml) red wine (or water) in a saucepan over low heat. Pit and quarter 1⅓ pounds (600g) plums. Add to the pan with 1 split vanilla bean and cook for 5 minutes, or until the plums begin to soften. Spoon the plums into the prepared baking dish with a slotted spoon. Simmer the remaining liquid until it has reduced by half, making a thick syrup. Remove the vanilla bean and drizzle the syrup over the plums before topping with the crumble.

Variations
Sugars: In place of the light brown sugar, use Demerara, superfine (caster), or granulated sugar in the crumble topping.

Topping texture: When adding the sugar, stir in any of these: 2½ tablespoons (25g) rolled oats; ½ cup (75g) chopped pecans, chopped hazelnuts, or slivered (flaked) almonds; 2 teaspoons of ground spices, such as cinnamon, nutmeg, or pumpkin pie spice (mixed spice).

Rachel's tip
Keep a large batch of the crumble mixture in a food bag in the freezer. Even when frozen, it will easily crumble, so you can remove handfuls to use straight away as you need it.

Rhubarb and ginger bread and butter pudding

Vegetarian

Serves 4 to 6

Preparation time: 30 minutes

Cooking time: 50 minutes

Ready in 2 hours

1 pound (450g) rhubarb stalks, cut into ½-inch (1cm) slices

4 teaspoons finely grated fresh ginger

¾ cup (150g) superfine (caster) or granulated sugar

4 tablespoons (50g) butter, softened

12 slices white sandwich bread, crusts removed

1½ cups (350ml) light or heavy (single or double) cream

1½ cups (350ml) milk

4 eggs

Pinch of salt

2 tablespoons granulated sugar

Confectioners' (icing) sugar, to serve

Softly whipped cream, to serve

This variation on the classic bread and butter pudding uses rhubarb and ginger, which go together so well. You can use fresh or frozen rhubarb and enjoy the pudding year-round.

For me and so many people in Ireland, this is the absolute essence of comfort food: a dessert that brings us all back to our childhoods, to memories of a dish that is best when cooked without precision or fussiness. It is unashamedly indulgent—the bread soaks up the custard while the sprinkling of granulated sugar ensures the top is perfectly crisp.

Rhubarb is something that grows really well in Ireland, and I have quite a prolific patch in my garden. I like to stew it simply with sugar and water, then serve it with yogurt or custard. This pudding is a serious treat.

Scatter the rhubarb in a 10-inch (25cm) square baking dish, and sprinkle with half the grated ginger and half the superfine sugar. Toss together and then let sit for about 30 minutes to soften a little.

Preheat the oven to 350°F (180°C/Gas mark 4). Butter the bread and arrange four slices, buttered side down, in the ovenproof dish. Scatter over half of the prepared rhubarb and top with four more slices of bread, again buttered side down. Repeat with the remaining rhubarb mixture and bread.

Combine the cream, milk, and remaining grated ginger in a saucepan and bring just to a boil. While this is coming to a boil, whisk the eggs, salt, and remaining superfine sugar in a bowl. Continuing to whisk, pour the hot liquid into the egg mixture until well mixed. Slowly pour this custard over the bread and let soak for 10 minutes. Sprinkle the granulated sugar over the top.

Place the baking dish in a roasting pan and pour in enough boiling water to come halfway up the sides (making a bain-marie). Carefully place in the oven and bake for 45 to 50 minutes, until the pudding feels just set in the center. Serve warm with a light dusting of confectioners' sugar and whipped cream.

Carrageen moss pudding with poached rhubarb

Vegetarian

Serves 4 to 6

Preparation time: 15 minutes

Cooking time: 20 minutes

Ready in 2½ hours

¼ ounce (7g) or 1 fistful Irish moss (carrageen) (don't use too much or the pudding will be too firm and strong in flavor)

4 cups (900ml) milk

4 tablespoons (50g) superfine (caster) or granulated sugar

1 egg, separated

1 teaspoon vanilla extract (essence)

½ cup (100ml) water

1 cup (225g) granulated sugar

1 pound (450g) rhubarb, stalks trimmed and cut into ¾-inch (2cm) chunks

I was first introduced to carrageen (carraigín in Irish, meaning "little rock") moss pudding—Irish moss pudding—when I came down to Ballymaloe at the age of 18. Myrtle Allen, who first opened the Ballymaloe House in 1964, has been cooking this dish in the restaurant for decades. It is an old Irish dish but hers is undoubtedly the best version I've tried. Carrageen is a type of seaweed that works like gelatin, and it gently sets the cooked milk to make a light and fluffy pudding. Carrageen is harvested at low tide, then put out to dry on the rocks. High in iodine and vitamins, it is also used in a traditional recipe for cough syrup that Myrtle Allen still makes and that she swears by. You can buy Irish moss in health food stores and online.

Soak the Irish moss in lukewarm water for 10 minutes, then drain and combine in a saucepan with the milk. Bring to a boil, then simmer over very low heat for 20 minutes.

Pour the milk through a sieve into a bowl. The Irish moss will now be swollen and resembling a jellyfish, so push the jelly through the sieve into the milk. Discard the remaining Irish moss. Whisk in the superfine sugar, egg yolk, and vanilla.

Whisk the egg white until stiff and gently stir it into the milk; it will rise to give the pudding a light, fluffy top. Pour into one large bowl or evenly distribute into individual cups or glasses. Cover and place in the fridge for 1 to 2 hours to set.

To poach the rhubarb, combine the water and granulated sugar in a saucepan, stir, and bring to a boil. Add the rhubarb, cover, bring to a boil, and simmer for exactly 1 minute. Turn off the heat and allow the rhubarb to remain in the covered saucepan until almost cool. Transfer to a bowl to finish cooling.

Serve the rhubarb on top of or on the side of the carrageen moss pudding.

Porter cake

Vegetarian

Serves 10 to 12

Preparation time: 30 minutes

Cooking time: 2 hours

Ready in 3 hours

3½ cups (450g) all-purpose (plain) flour

1 teaspoon grated or ground nutmeg

1 teaspoon pumpkin pie spice (mixed spice)

1 teaspoon baking powder

Pinch of salt

1 cup (225g) butter

1 cup packed (225g) light brown sugar

1 pound (450g) golden raisins (sultanas) or raisins or a mixture of both

3 ounces (75g) chopped candied peel, store-bought or homemade (see page 202)

2 eggs

1 (12-ounce/330ml) bottle porter or stout

This traditional Irish cake uses a porter, such as Guinness, Beamish, or Murphy's, and is a deliciously rich and moist fruit cake. Make it a few days in advance of the celebratory event (it's perfect for St Patrick's Day) if you wish, and it will improve even more!

Preheat the oven to 350°F (180°C/Gas mark 4). Line the sides and bottom of an 8-inch (20cm) high-sided round cake pan (the sides should be about 2¾ inches/7cm high) with waxed (greaseproof) paper.

Sift the flour, nutmeg, spice, baking powder, and salt into a bowl. Rub in the butter, then stir in the brown sugar, raisins, and candied peel.

Whisk the eggs in another bowl and add the porter. Pour into the dry ingredients and mix well. Pour into the prepared pan.

Bake for about 2 hours. If the cake starts to brown too quickly on top, cover it with aluminum foil or waxed (greaseproof) paper after about 1 hour. The cake is done when a skewer inserted into the center comes out clean. Allow the cake to sit in the pan for about 20 minutes before turning it out and cooling it on a wire rack.

Christmas pudding with whiskey cream

Vegetarian

Serves 8 to 12

Preparation time: 40 minutes

Cooking time: 3 hours

Ready in 5 hours

⅔ cup (100g) raisins

⅔ cup (100g) golden raisins (sultanas)

⅔ cup (100g) dried cranberries

3½ ounces (100g) candied peel, store-bought or homemade (page 202), chopped

⅔ cup (100g) dried currants

4 dates (pitted) (100g), halved

½ cup (100ml) whiskey, plus extra for serving

1 cup (100g) ground almonds

2 cooking apples, such as Bramley or Granny Smith, grated (do not peel)

Finely grated zest and juice of 1 lemon

6 tablespoons golden syrup (or substitute dark corn syrup)

10 whole, blanched (skinned) almonds

14 tablespoons (200g) butter, chilled and grated

¾ cup packed (180g) dark brown sugar

4 eggs, beaten

1¾ cups (230g) gluten-free flour, or 2 cups (250g) self-rising flour, sifted

½ teaspoon baking powder

¼ whole nutmeg, finely grated

½ teaspoon ground cinnamon

ingredients continue overleaf

When I was growing up, our Christmas pudding would vary a little each year. My mum didn't use exact quantities of anything, and I liked that each year was different. I'm like that myself, adding a little more or less of some ingredients some of the times. I love the not-so-traditional cranberries in this recipe, which give the pudding a delightfully zingy flavor.

In a saucepan, gently simmer the dried fruit in the whiskey for 3 minutes. Remove from the heat, cover, and leave for at least 1 hour.

Mix the ground almonds, apples, and lemon zest and juice together in a bowl.

Set out two (5-cup/1l) pudding basins or deep, heatproof bowls, preferably ceramic. Pour 3 tablespoons of golden syrup into each of the pudding basins and arrange 5 almonds and a few pieces of soaked fruit decoratively in the golden syrup.

Using a wooden or metal spoon, mix the grated butter, brown sugar, and eggs together in a large bowl. Add the flour, baking powder, nutmeg, and cinnamon and mix together thoroughly. Spoon into the pudding basins and flatten out. Gently bang the bowls on the work surface to release any air bubbles.

Cut two rounds of parchment paper to fit neatly over the top of each, then cut out two more rounds about ¼ inch (5mm) wider than the rim of the basin. Place them over the basins and tie with a long piece of string under the lip of the bowl and over the top again. Tie at the other side to make a handle.

Place each basin in a large saucepan and carefully pour hot water around them to come three-quarters of the way up the sides. Cover and steam for 3 hours, keeping the water in the saucepan topped up all the time.

Remove the basins from the water and allow to cool. Remove the top paper lid and cover with a new one. Store in a cool place.

recipe continues overleaf

½ cup (100ml) heavy (double) cream

1 to 2 tablespoons confectioners' (icing) sugar, sifted

2 tablespoons Irish whiskey

Finely grated zest of 1 small orange

Reheat by steaming for 1 hour in the same way as above. Meanwhile, make the whiskey orange cream. Whip the cream until just stiff and fold in the confectioners' sugar, whiskey, and orange zest.

To serve, turn the puddings out onto a large platter. Pour a little whiskey over and ignite. Serve with the whiskey orange cream.

Candied peel

Vegetarian

Makes about 4½ cups (1.1l)

Preparation time: 30 minutes plus 24 hours soaking

Cooking time: 4 hours plus 30 minutes cooling

5 oranges

5 lemons

5 grapefruit

1 teaspoon salt

6¼ cups (1.25kg) superfine (caster) or granulated sugar

You can use the mixture of fruit suggested here, or just fifteen of the same fruit.

Cut the fruit in half and squeeze out the juice. (Reserve the juice for another use, perhaps homemade lemonade.) Put the peel into a large bowl, add the salt, and cover with cold water. Leave to soak for 24 hours.

Next day, throw away the soaking water, put the peel in a large saucepan and cover with fresh cold water. Bring to a boil, cover, and simmer very gently for about 3 hours, or until the peel is soft. It should mash between the tips of your fingers easily when it is cooked. Remove the peel from the pan and discard the water. Scrape out any remaining flesh and membrane from inside the cut fruit, using a teaspoon, leaving the white pith and rind intact.

In a clean large saucepan, dissolve the sugar in 4¼ cups (1l) of water, then bring to a boil, stirring to dissolve the sugar. Add the peel and simmer gently for 30 to 60 minutes until it looks shiny and translucent ("candied") and the syrup forms a thread when the last drop falls off a metal spoon. Remove from the heat and allow to stand for 20 to 30 minutes to cool slightly.

Put the candied peel into sterilized glass jars (see page 188) and pour the syrup over. Cover and store in a cold place or in the fridge. It should keep, stored like this, for at least 3 months. You can chop or slice the candied peel as you need it.

St. Stephen's Day muffins

Vegetarian

Makes 6 muffins

Preparation time: 20 minutes

Cooking time: 25 minutes

Ready in 1 hour

1 egg

6 tablespoons milk

2 tablespoons (25g) butter, melted

2 tablespoons sherry, Irish whiskey, or brandy

½ cup (125g) leftover Christmas pudding (page 200), broken into lumps

1 cup (125g) all-purpose (plain) flour

1 teaspoon baking powder

½ teaspoon pumpkin pie spice (mixed spice)

6 tablespoons (75g) superfine (caster) or granulated sugar

Confectioners' (icing) sugar, for dusting

St. Stephen's Day, as it is known in Ireland, is the day after Christmas. And what better way to use up any bits of leftover Christmas pudding than with these festive and delicious muffins? They are divine with a cup of coffee or tea and can be frozen.

Preheat the oven to 350°F (180°C/Gas mark 4). Line a 12-cup muffin pan or 24-cup mini muffin pan with paper liners.

Whisk the egg in a bowl, then add the milk, melted butter, sherry, and the pieces of Christmas pudding.

Sift the flour, baking powder, and pumpkin pie spice into another bowl. Add the superfine sugar and mix well. Make a well in the center, add the wet ingredients, and mix together until a soft, lumpy batter forms.

Spoon the mixture into the paper liners and bake for 20 to 25 minutes, until the muffins feel springy to the touch.

Allow to cool in the pan for a few minutes, then remove from the pan and place on a wire rack to cool completely. Dust with confectioners' sugar to serve.

Irish coffee meringue roulade

Vegetarian

Serves 6 to 8

Preparation time: 30 minutes

Cooking time: 25 to 30 minutes

Ready in 2 hours

A little vegetable oil, for greasing

4 egg whites

1 cup (225g) superfine (caster) or granulated sugar

1 tablespoon instant coffee powder

FOR THE FILLING

1¾ cups (425ml) whipping cream

1 teaspoon instant coffee powder

1 tablespoon sifted confectioners' (icing) sugar, plus extra for dusting

2 tablespoons Irish whiskey

This Irish coffee roulade is quite a grown-up dessert. It's decidedly wintery, and I like to make it when there's not much fresh fruit around. Of course, the Irish know just how well whiskey and coffee go together, and this dish is perfect served with small Irish Coffees (page 210).

Preheat the oven to 350°F (180°C/Gas mark 4). Line a 9 by 13-inch (23 by 33cm) jelly roll pan with aluminum foil, folding the sides up to make a frame 1½ inches (4cm) high and squeezing the corners together. Brush lightly with vegetable oil.

Put the egg whites in the spotlessly clean bowl (stainless steel is best) of an electric stand mixer (or use a handheld electric beater) and whisk until soft peaks form.

Add the sugar all in one go (but if using a handheld beater, add the sugar in stages) and whisk at full speed for 4 to 5 minutes, until stiff peaks form. Using a large metal spoon, fold in the instant coffee firmly and quickly. Spoon the meringue into the prepared pan and smooth with a spatula.

Bake for 15 to 20 minutes, until faintly browned and firm to the touch.

Allow the meringue to cool for a few minutes, then turn out onto a sheet of foil (slightly bigger than the roulade), carefully turning it upside down onto the sheet and gently removing the foil on the bottom. Allow to cool completely.

To make the filling, whip the cream until it forms soft peaks, then fold in the instant coffee, confectioners' sugar, and whiskey. Spread the coffee cream over the meringue, leaving the long edge nearest to you free of cream for about 1½ inches (4cm).

Holding the foil closest to you, roll up the roulade away from you and leave it in the foil until you are ready to serve (it will hold neatly here for a couple of hours in the fridge).

When ready to serve, unwrap the roulade and gently push it onto a serving dish using a spatula. Dust with confectioners' sugar and serve immediately.

Irish coffee cups

Vegetarian

Serves 4

Preparation time: 30 minutes

Cooking time: 25 to 30 minutes

Ready in 2 hours

9 tablespoons (125g) butter, softened

½ cup packed (125g) light brown sugar

2 eggs

1 tablespoon coffee extract (essence) (ideally Camp or Irel brand)

1 cup (125g) all-purpose (plain) flour

1 teaspoon baking powder

⅔ cup (150ml) heavy or whipping (double or regular) cream, softly whipped, to serve

FOR THE SAUCE

10 tablespoons (125g) superfine (caster) or granulated sugar

6 tablespoons water

⅔ cup (150ml) heavy or whipping (double or regular) cream

4 tablespoons Irish whiskey

Warm coffee cakes served in teacups with a whiskey sauce and whipped cream, these make a smart and playful dessert, perfect for a dinner party, because both the cakes and sauce can be made ahead of time. The cakes are better if made on the same day, but the sauce can be made up to a couple of days ahead. Reheat the sauce in a saucepan and reheat the cakes in the oven (preheated to 250°F/130°C/Gas mark ½) for 10 minutes or just until warmed through. Serve with Irish coffee (page 210).

Preheat the oven to 350°F (180°C/Gas mark 4), and butter the insides of four small ovenproof teacups or four 2½-inch (6cm) diameter ramekins, if you intend to tip the cakes out of them for serving.

Cream the butter until soft in a large bowl or with an electric stand mixer with the paddle attachment. Add the brown sugar and beat until the mixture is light and fluffy.

Whisk the eggs with the coffee extract in a small bowl for just a few seconds until mixed, then gradually add to the creamed butter mixture, beating all the time. Sift in the flour and baking powder and fold in gently to combine.

Divide the mixture among the teacups or ramekins and place these in a deep-sided ovenproof dish or roasting pan. Pour boiling water into the dish so it comes to halfway up the sides of the cups.

Bake for 25 to 30 minutes, until the center of each cake is springy to the touch.

While the cakes are baking, make the sauce. Combine the superfine sugar and water in a saucepan and bring to a boil, stirring to dissolve the sugar as the mixture heats up. Turn the heat up to high and continue to boil, but without stirring, until the syrup becomes a deep golden caramel color. Cook the sauce just to the point when it starts smoking. (If it's not cooked enough you won't get a strong enough caramel flavor, but if overcooked it will taste slightly bitter.) You may need to swirl the pan, rather than stirring the mixture, toward the end of caramelizing to ensure it cooks evenly.

recipe continues overleaf

Turn down the heat and immediately stir in the cream and whiskey, taking care as it may bubble and spit; then set aside. You may need to whisk it for a few seconds over low heat to help the caramel dissolve into the cream and whiskey.

When the cakes are done, remove from the oven and allow to cool for a couple of minutes. Place on saucers or serving plates, or tip them out onto warm plates if you prefer. To serve, pour a tablespoon of the warm whiskey sauce over each, then top that with a spoonful of softly whipped cream.

Irish coffee

Vegetarian

Serves 1

Preparation time: 5 minutes

2 tablespoons plus 1 teaspoon Irish whiskey (Paddy's, Powers, or Jameson)

1½ teaspoons brown sugar

Hot coffee

Softly whipped cream

Irish coffee was invented by Joe Sheridan at what was then Shannon Airport in 1942. The story goes that on a particularly stormy evening, one plane was lucky to land, and Joe Sheridan, the chef at the airport's restaurant, wanted to make a drink to warm them through. He added Irish whiskey to a sweetened coffee with cream. One of the passengers asked if they were drinking Brazilian coffee, and Joe replied that it was Irish coffee. The drink is now universally popular and still served all over Ireland.

The trick with Irish coffee is that there must be enough sugar in the coffee to support the weight of the cream. If there's not enough sugar, the cream sinks to the bottom. The cream shouldn't hold a stiff peak, but should hold a very soft peak.

Pour the whiskey into a cup and stir in the brown sugar. Top up with coffee, leaving a space of ½ inch (1cm) from the rim of the cup to the top of the coffee, and stir to dissolve the sugar. Dip a spoon into hot or boiling water, then use that spoon to add the cream to the coffee—it will slide gently off the spoon.

Little hot after-dinner shots

Vegetarian

Serves 8

Preparation time: 5 minutes

Cooking time: 3 minutes

¾ cup (200ml) brandy or whiskey

¾ cup (200ml) Simple Syrup
(see below)

8 tablespoons softly whipped cream

Merrilees Parker, a wonderful cook from the UK, made something similar to this when I appeared with her on the television show Great Food Live. I like to serve this after a winter dinner party. It is nicely luxurious—a little like Irish coffee, only without the coffee!

Pour the brandy and syrup into a saucepan and heat very gently; do not boil. Divide among eight little glasses. Dip a spoon into boiling water and use to spoon on the cream, allowing it to slide off the spoon and sit on top of the sweet brandy or whiskey. The cream should not sink. Serve immediately.

Simple syrup

Vegetarian

Makes ⅔ cup (150ml)

Preparation time: 5 minutes

1 cup (200g) superfine (caster) or
granulated sugar

¾ cup (200ml) water

This basic sugar syrup (called stock syrup in Ireland) has many uses, including sweetening cocktails and poaching fruit. It keeps indefinitely, and it is very handy to have some on hand.

Combine the sugar and water in a saucepan and bring slowly to a boil, stirring to dissolve the sugar. When the sugar has dissolved, boil for 2 minutes and allow to cool.

Steamed ginger treacle pudding

Vegetarian

Serves 6

Preparation time: 30 minutes

Cooking time: 1½ hours

Ready in 2 hours

½ cup (125g) butter, diced and softened, plus extra for greasing

4 tablespoons treacle (or substitute molasses)

4 tablespoons ginger syrup (from the stem ginger jar, or substitute golden syrup or corn syrup)

½ cup packed (110g) light brown sugar

2 eggs

1¼ cups (150g) self-rising flour, sifted

2 tablespoons milk

4 tablespoons (75g) stem ginger, very finely chopped

Ice cream, softly whipped cream, or custard (page 182), to serve

This pudding is really just a hug in a bowl. The glorious steamed pudding is made perfectly sweet with the toffeelike flavor of treacle and the gentle heat of ginger. You can buy stem ginger in syrup online if you can't find it elsewhere. Alternatively, you can use crystallized ginger in the cake batter and then golden syrup (or corn syrup) in place of the ginger syrup in the treacle mix.

Butter a 5-cup (1l) pudding basin or deep, heatproof bowl, preferably ceramic. Mix the treacle and the stem ginger syrup together and pour into the bottom of the basin.

Cream the butter and brown sugar together by hand or with an electric stand mixer with the paddle attachment until light and fluffy. Beat in the eggs, one at a time. Fold in the flour and add in the milk. Stir in the stem ginger and spoon the mixture into the pudding basin to fill it two-thirds of the way up, smoothing the top with the back of the spoon. (The treacle will come up the inside of the basin, so be careful not to mix it into the cake mixture.)

Butter a piece of waxed (greaseproof) paper and fold a pleat across the center. Cover the basin with the paper, butter side down, and secure with string under the lip of the basin (see page 200). Place in a steamer with a tight-fitting lid and simmer over low heat for 1¼ to 1½ hours, until the top of the pudding is firm to the touch and a skewer inserted into the middle comes out clean. Remember to top up the water in the steamer, if necessary.

Alternatively, if you don't have a steamer, sit the pudding basin on an upturned saucer in the bottom of a large saucepan. Pour enough boiling water to come halfway up the sides of the basin, and cover with a tight-fitting lid, then cook for the same length of time. Again, remember to keep the water topped up all the time.

Remove the pudding basin from the steamer, carefully loosen the pudding by running a spatula around the inside of the basin, and invert onto a warm serving plate (one that is wider than the top of the basin). The treacle sauce will ooze down the sides of the pudding. Spoon over any sauce remaining in the basin and serve with ice cream, whipped cream, or custard.

Dark sticky gingerbread

Vegetarian

Makes 1 loaf

Preparation time: 20 minutes

Cooking time: 55 minutes

Ready in 1 hour 40 minutes

5 tablespoons (60g) butter

¼ cup (75g) golden syrup (or substitute dark corn syrup)

2 tablespoons plus 1 teaspoon (50g) molasses or black treacle

¾ cup (110g) all-purpose (plain) flour

4 tablespoons (25g) self-rising flour

1 teaspoon baking soda (bicarbonate of soda)

1 heaping teaspoon ground ginger

1 teaspoon ground cinnamon

1 teaspoon freshly grated nutmeg

1 teaspoon freshly ground black pepper

½ cup (100g) superfine (caster) or granulated sugar

Pinch of salt

½ cup (120ml) milk

1 egg, beaten

2 ounces (50g) crystallized ginger, finely chopped

FOR THE SYRUP

6½ tablespoons (80g) superfine (caster) or granulated sugar

⅓ cup (80ml) water

1 teaspoon finely grated fresh ginger

FOR THE TOPPING (OPTIONAL)

1⅔ cups (200g) confectioners' (icing) sugar, sifted

Juice of ½ lemon

This classic teatime cake can be served warm with cream as a dessert or sliced and buttered at any time. The flavor is quite intense, and it's the kind of treat that is immensely satisfying. It stays deliciously moist and has a lovely mixture of different spices so will keep very well. Divine with a cup of coffee.

Preheat the oven to 325°F (170°C /Gas Mark 3). Line a 5 by 9-inch (13 by 23cm) loaf pan with parchment paper.

Melt the butter, golden syrup, and molasses in a small saucepan over low heat. Set aside.

Sift the flours, baking soda, ginger, cinnamon, nutmeg, and pepper into a large bowl. Stir in the sugar and salt. Add the milk and egg and mix until smooth. Gradually add the melted butter mixture, stirring until well incorporated. Fold in the chopped crystallized ginger. The mixture will be runny. Pour into the prepared loaf pan.

Bake for 50 to 55 minutes, until risen and firm to the touch, and a skewer inserted into the middle comes out clean. Do not open the oven to test before the bread has baked for at least 45 minutes.

After the gingerbread has been baking for about 40 minutes, make the syrup. Combine the sugar, water, and grated ginger in a small saucepan and simmer for 10 minutes. When the gingerbread is done, remove from the oven and prick all over with a fine skewer. Pour over the hot syrup, then place the cake pan on a wire rack to cool for 20 minutes. Remove the cake from the pan and place on a wire rack to cool completely.

To make the topping, mix together the confectioners' sugar and lemon juice in a small bowl until thick and smooth. Spread carefully over the top of the cake with a spatula or a table knife, allowing some icing to drip over the edges.

Brown bread ice cream

Vegetarian

Serves 6 to 8

Preparation time: 30 minutes

Cooking time: 15 minutes

Ready in 12 hours

1½ cups (100g) chopped Brown Soda Bread (page 227) or Brown Yeast Bread (page 230)

¼ cup packed (50g) brown sugar

¼ teaspoon ground cinnamon

⅔ cup (150ml) whipping or heavy (double) cream

2 eggs, separated

1 tablespoon rum (optional)

½ cup (125g) granulated sugar

½ cup (100ml) water

Pinch of cream of tartar

It may seem strange, but this Victorian invention is a divine ice cream. It's a wonderful way of using our great Irish bread, whether it's brown soda bread or brown yeast bread. The crumbs are mixed with sugar and caramelized in the oven. The deeply flavored sweet nuggets are then stirred into the rich ice cream. This is perfect on its own or with a butterscotch, caramel, or chocolate sauce (page 220).

This recipe is particularly useful as it doesn't require an ice cream machine; you simply stir the cream into an Italian meringue, then freeze it overnight. The ice cream it makes is very light and doesn't need to soften before scooping.

Preheat the oven to 400°F (200°C/Gas mark 6).

Place the bread in a food processor and whiz for 30 to 60 seconds to form coarse bread crumbs. Add the brown sugar and cinnamon and pulse for a few times just to mix. Spread out on a baking sheet and toast in the oven for about 10 minutes, until well browned. Remove from the oven and set aside to cool.

Whisk the cream until soft peaks appear, then mix in the egg yolks and rum (if using) and set aside.

Combine the granulated sugar and water in a saucepan and heat slowly, stirring to dissolve the sugar. Increase the heat to high and bring to a boil. Boil fiercely for 5 minutes, until the syrup thickens and the last drops on a spoon dipped into it form a sort of thread. Meanwhile, using an electric whisk, whisk the egg whites with the cream of tartar until stiff. Still whisking, gradually pour in the hot syrup in a thin stream, and continue to whisk until the mixture is cool, glossy, and stiff, 4 to 5 minutes. Add the whipped cream mixture along with the caramelized bread crumbs and fold until mixed through.

Transfer the mixture to a container with a lid, cover, and place in the freezer. Freeze overnight before serving.

Dark chocolate sauce

Vegetarian

Makes ¾ cup (175ml)

Preparation time: 5 minutes

Cooking time: 5 minutes

½ cup (75g) chopped dark chocolate

½ cup (100ml) heavy or whipping (double or regular) cream

Very quick to make, this hot chocolate sauce is the ultimate in sinfulness—perfect drizzled over any ice cream, especially the Brown Bread Ice Cream (page 218). Although it keeps in the fridge for several weeks, I challenge you to leave it there for that long.

Melt the chocolate in a heatproof bowl sitting over a saucepan of gently simmering water. Whisk in the cream to make a smooth sauce. Keep warm in the bowl until ready to serve.

Breads and cookies

Fresh bread, whether soda or yeast, is a pleasure to have, both to serve
with other food and for the wonderful aromas that fill the kitchen.
Soda bread is the quintessential Irish bread. It has long been made in
home kitchens and restaurants everywhere and is still to this day. While
soda bread is quick to put together, I also adore bread made with yeast,
though it takes a little more time.

This chapter also has a number of different recipes for cookies (which we
call biscuits) and fruit breads, the sweet treats that I often bake to serve
with tea or coffee.

Soda bread

Vegetarian

Makes 1 loaf

Preparation time: 10 minutes

Cooking time: 45 minutes

Ready in 1 hour 10 minutes

3½ cups (450g) all-purpose (plain) flour, plus extra for dusting

1 teaspoon superfine (caster) or granulated sugar

1 teaspoon baking soda (bicarbonate of soda)

1 teaspoon salt

1½ to 2 cups (350–425ml) buttermilk or soured milk (see tip, page 228)

This traditional Irish loaf is one of the fastest bread recipes to make.

Preheat the oven to 450°F (230°C/Gas mark 8).

Sift the flour, sugar, baking soda, and salt into a large bowl. Make a well in the center and pour in most of the buttermilk, leaving about ¼ cup (50ml) in the measuring cup. Using one hand with your fingers outstretched like a claw, bring the flour and liquid together, adding more buttermilk, if necessary. Don't knead the mixture, or it will become heavy. The dough should be soft, but not too wet and sticky.

When the dough comes together, turn it onto a floured work surface and bring it together a little more. Pat the dough into a round about 1½ inches (4cm) thick and cut a deep cross in it. Place on a baking sheet.

Bake for 15 minutes. Turn down the heat to 400°F (200°C/Gas mark 6) and bake for 30 minutes more. When done, the loaf will sound slightly hollow when tapped on the bottom and be golden in color. I often turn it upside down for the last 5 minutes of cooking. Allow to cool on a wire rack.

Brown soda bread

Vegetarian

Makes 1 loaf

Preparation time: 10 minutes

Cooking time: 45 minutes

Ready in 1 hour 10 minutes

1¾ cups (225g) whole wheat (wholemeal) flour

1¾ cups (225g) all-purpose (plain) flour

1 teaspoon salt

1 teaspoon baking soda (bicarbonate of soda)

3 tablespoons (50g) mixed seeds, such as sesame, pumpkin, or sunflower, or golden flax seeds (linseeds) (optional)

2 tablespoons (25g) butter, softened (optional)

1 egg

About 1⅔ cups (375–400ml) buttermilk or soured milk (see tip, page 228)

Soda bread is quintessentially Irish and still made fresh in people's kitchens every day. It is so easy to make and is absolutely at its best eaten the day it's made. The bicarbonate of soda or baking soda (called "bread soda" in Ireland) is the leavening agent, reacting with the buttermilk to produce bubbles of carbon dioxide and leaven the bread. We eat brown soda bread with many different foods, but it is especially good with smoked salmon and mackerel and with hard cheese and chutney.

Preheat the oven to 425°F (220°C/Gas mark 7).

Sift together the flours, salt, and baking soda in a large bowl and mix in the seeds (if using). Add the butter (if using), and rub into the flour mixture with your fingertips until it resembles bread crumbs. Make a well in the center.

In another bowl, whisk the egg with the buttermilk and pour most of the liquid into the flour mixture. Using one hand with your fingers outstretched like a claw, bring the flour and liquid together, adding more of the buttermilk mixture, if necessary. The dough should be quite soft, but not too sticky.

Turn onto a floured work surface and gently bring the dough together into a round about 1½ inches (4cm) thick. Cut a deep cross on top and place on a baking sheet.

Bake for 15 minutes. Turn down the heat to 400°F (200°C/Gas mark 6) and bake for 30 minutes more. When done, the loaf will sound slightly hollow when tapped on the bottom. Remove from the baking sheet and place on a wire rack to cool.

Cheesy soda scones

Vegetarian

Makes about 16 scones

Preparation time: 10 minutes

Cooking time: 20 minutes

Ready in 50 minutes

3½ cups (450g) all-purpose (plain) white flour

1 teaspoon salt

1 teaspoon baking soda (bicarbonate of soda)

1 tablespoon chopped fresh herbs, such as rosemary, thyme, sage, parsley, or chives

1⅔ cups (400ml) buttermilk or soured milk (see tip)

⅔ cup (75g) grated cheddar or Gruyère cheese

All children love playing with dough, and with this Irish soda bread dough you can be as creative as you like. I often leave out the herbs; sometimes I leave out the cheese and replace the herbs with a handful of chopped milk or dark chocolate, or even raisins or dried cranberries. These scones can be cut into any shapes that your little ones like, though if handled and kneaded too much, they will get slightly tough.

Preheat the oven to 475°F (250°C/Gas mark 9). Flour a baking sheet.

Sift the flour, salt, and baking soda into a bowl. Mix in the herbs. Make a well in the center. Pour in all the buttermilk at once. Using one hand, with your fingers outstretched like a claw, stir in a full circular movement from the center to the outside of the bowl to form a dough. The dough should be soft, though not too wet and sticky.

When the dough comes together, turn it out onto a well-floured surface. Pat the dough until it is about ¾ inch (2cm) thick. Cut into sixteen round or square shapes and place on the prepared baking sheet. Generously sprinkle each scone with the grated cheese.

Bake for about 15 minutes, until golden and sounding hollow when tapped on the bottom. Turn the oven down to 400°F (200°C/Gas mark 6) after 10 minutes if they are already golden. Remove from the baking sheet and place on a wire rack to cool slightly before serving.

Variations

To make chocolate chip soda scones, omit the cheese and replace the herbs with ⅓ cup (75g) of chopped dark or milk chocolate or chocolate chips. You could also add an egg to the buttermilk and 1 tablespoon superfine (caster) or granulated sugar to increase the richness. It's also delicious with ¾ cup (100g) raisins or dried cranberries.

Rachel's tip

To make your own soured milk, gently heat milk (the quantity required for the recipe) until warm. Remove from the heat, add the juice of ½ lemon and leave at room temperature overnight. If you are allergic to dairy products, this recipe works well with soy milk or rice milk soured in the same way.

Ballymaloe brown yeast bread

Vegetarian

Makes 1 loaf

Preparation time: 10 minutes

Cooking time: 1 hour

Ready in 1¾ hours

A little vegetable oil for greasing

3¾ cups (450g) whole wheat (wholemeal) flour or 3⅓ cups (400g) whole wheat (wholemeal) flour plus ⅓ cup (50g) white bread (strong white) flour

1 teaspoon salt

1 teaspoon black treacle or molasses

1¾ cups (425ml) lukewarm water

1 ounce (25g) fresh yeast or 2 (¼-ounce/7g) packets active dry baking yeast

1 tablespoon sesame, poppy, or sunflower seeds (optional)

This brown yeast bread is a version of Doris Grant's no-knead brown bread as made by my grandmother-in-law, Myrtle Allen. Because it isn't kneaded, this bread only takes minutes to make and is full of the divinely nutty whole-grain flavor. If you'd like a slightly lighter loaf, you can substitute white bread flour for some of the whole wheat flour. You can also add a sprinkling of seeds for nutty flavor and added nutrition.

This bread has a distinctive flavor that works well with other strong flavors and is the perfect bread to serve with smoked fish.

Preheat the oven to 425°F (220°C/Gas mark 7). Grease a 9 by 5-inch (23 by 13cm) loaf pan with vegetable oil. Make sure all of the ingredients are at room temperature.

Mix the flour with the salt. In a small bowl or Pyrex measuring cup, mix the treacle with ⅔ cup (150ml) of the lukewarm water and add in the yeast. Let sit for a few minutes in a warm place to allow the yeast to start to work. After 4 or 5 minutes, it should have a creamy, slightly frothy appearance.

When the yeast is ready, stir and pour it, with all the remaining water, into the flour to make a loose sloppy dough. The mixture should be too wet to knead. Put the mixture into the greased loaf pan. If using the seeds, sprinkle them over the dough now. Lay a kitchen towel over the top of the pan. Leave on your work surface to rise to the top of the pan. It will take from 5 to 25 minutes to rise, depending on the temperature of the kitchen and the dough itself. Remove the towel and pop the loaf in the center of the oven. Look at the loaf after 20 minutes; if it is a deep brown, decrease the heat of the oven to 400°F (200°C/Gas mark 6). After 50 to 60 minutes, the loaf should look nicely browned and sound hollow when tapped. Remove from the oven, take out of the pan, and place on a wire rack to cool.

If you'd like a thicker crust, remove the loaf from the pan 10 minutes before the end of baking and place directly on an oven rack to bake for the last 10 minutes.

Wholemeal honey bread

Vegetarian

Makes 2 loaves

Preparation time: 30 minutes

Cooking time: 40 minutes

Ready in 4 hours

2 cups (450ml) warm water

3 tablespoons honey

1 tablespoon active dry baking yeast or fast-acting baking yeast or 1¾ ounces (40g) fresh yeast

4⅓ cups (600g) white bread (strong white) flour

2½ cups (300g) whole wheat (wholemeal) flour

2 teaspoons salt

½ cup (100g) butter, cut into ½-inch (1cm) cubes

Making yeast bread from scratch is becoming a lost art, but it is the perfect thing to do with your children—to teach new skills and to have fun. This is a simple and tasty bread, and once you have mastered it, you'll want to move on to other flavors and combinations.

In a small bowl, mix the warm water with the honey; add the yeast and let stand for 5 minutes until slightly frothy.

Combine the flours in a big mixing bowl or in the bowl of an electric stand mixer fitted with the dough hook attachment and mix in the salt. Rub in the butter. Pour most of the frothy liquid into the flour and mix to form a dough. If it's too dry and feels floury, add a little more warm water; if it feels very wet and sticky, add a little more flour.

Knead by hand on a floured surface or in the mixer for about 10 minutes (it may only take 5 minutes in the mixer), until the dough is smooth and springy. Place in a large oiled bowl, cover with plastic wrap (cling film), and leave in a warm spot for 2 to 3 hours, until it's doubled in size and does not spring back when you push your finger into the dough.

Knock back the dough by punching it down in the bowl (my children love this bit!) and knead on the floured surface for 1 minute. Allow to rest on the work surface, covered with a kitchen towel, for 5 minutes.

I usually shape the dough into two round or oval loaves but, of course, you can make individual rolls if you wish (you will get about 20 rolls). Slash the loaves four or five times over the top with a sharp knife (I don't do this with rolls). Do make sure you flatten the loaves and rolls to about 1½ inches (4cm) in height because they will rise.

Preheat the oven to 400°F (200°C/Gas mark 6).

Place the loaves (or rolls) on a floured baking sheet, sprinkle with flour, cover with a kitchen towel, and let rise in a warm place until doubled in size, about 45 minutes. The dough has risen enough when it does not spring back when you push your finger onto it.

Remove the kitchen towel and bake the loaves for 30 to 40 minutes (bake rolls for 10 to 15 minutes), until a loaf sounds hollow when tapped on the bottom. Cool on a wire rack.

Spotted dog

Vegetarian

Makes 1 loaf

Preparation time: 10 minutes

Cooking time: 45 minutes

Ready in 1 hour 10 minutes

3⅔ cups (450g) all-purpose (plain) flour, plus extra for dusting

1 teaspoon baking soda (bicarbonate of soda)

1 teaspoon salt

1 tablespoon superfine (caster) or granulated sugar

⅔ cup (110g) golden raisins (sultanas), raisins, or dried currants (or a mixture)

1 egg

1⅔ cups (400ml) buttermilk or soured milk (see tip, page 228)

This is a rich white soda bread with dried fruit added to make it "spotted." A real family favorite of ours, it's divine served straight from the oven, cut into slices, and smothered in butter and jam, or toasted and topped with cheese.

Preheat the oven to 425°F (220°C/Gas mark 7). Lightly dust a baking sheet with flour.

Sift the flour, baking soda, and salt into a large bowl. Stir in the sugar and dried fruit.

In a separate bowl, beat together the egg and buttermilk. Make a well in the center of the dry ingredients and pour most of the buttermilk mixture (leaving about ¼ cup/50ml in the bowl).

Using one hand with your fingers outstretched like a claw, bring the flour and liquid together moving your hand in circles around the bowl, adding a little more of the buttermilk mixture, if necessary. Don't knead the mixture, or it will become too heavy. The dough should be soft, but not too wet and sticky.

Once it comes together, turn onto a floured work surface and bring together a little more. Pat the dough into a round, about 2½ inches (6cm) in height, and cut a deep cross in it, from one side of the loaf to the other. Transfer to the prepared baking sheet.

Bake for 10 minutes, then decrease the oven temperature to 400°F (200°C/Gas mark 6), and bake for another 30 to 35 minutes, until the bread is golden and sounds hollow when tapped on the bottom. I often turn the loaf upside down for the last 5 minutes of baking to help crisp the bottom. Allow to cool on a wire rack before cutting into thick slices to serve.

Variation

Spotted dog scones: Preheat the oven to 450°F (230°C/Gas mark 8). Make the spotted dog dough as above but flatten into a round about 1 inch (3cm) in height. Cut into scones using a cookie cutter or knife and bake for 15 to 20 minutes.

Barmbrack (báirín breac)

Vegetarian

Serves 8

Preparation time: 30 minutes

Cooking time: 45 minutes

Ready in 1¾ hours

1⅔ cups (225g) white bread (strong white) flour, plus extra for dusting

2 tablespoons pumpkin pie spice (mixed spice)

¼ teaspoon salt

2 tablespoons (25g) butter, plus extra for spreading

1 (¼-ounce/7g) package fast-rising baking yeast

¼ cup (50g) superfine (caster) or granulated sugar

⅔ cup (150ml) milk

1 egg, beaten

1½ cups (200g) mixed dried fruit, either ready-mixed or your own mixture of golden raisins (sultanas), raisins, and dried currants

1 ounce (25g) chopped mixed candied peel, store-bought or homemade (see page 202)

Barmbrack is a traditional Irish sweetened bread not dissimilar to the Welsh bara brith. In Gaelic it's known as báirín breac, or "speckled loaf" due to the way the dough is dotted with raisins. When barmbrack was baked for Halloween, the tradition was to add to the cake mixture a pea, a stick, a piece of cloth, a coin, and a ring. Each item had a special significance for the person who discovered it in their slice of cake. The person who received the pea wouldn't marry that year; the stick meant an unhappy marriage; the cloth indicated poverty and the coin riches; while the person who found the ring would wed within the year. Nowadays it's usually just a ring that's added to the batter. The cake is delicious toasted and buttered and, if not immediately consumed, will keep for about 10 days.

This is a relatively quick recipe for barmbrack because it uses fast-action yeast, requiring the dough to rise only once.

Butter the sides and the bottom of a 9 by 5-inch (23 by 13cm) loaf pan.

Sift the flour, spice, and salt into a large bowl and add the butter, yeast, and sugar. Beat together by hand or in a stand mixer fitted with a dough hook attachment.

Warm the milk just until lukewarm, then add to the flour mixture along with the egg. Mix until the dough comes together. Then knead using a dough hook in an electric mixer, or tip the dough out onto a well-floured work surface and knead by hand (don't worry this is supposed to be a wet dough). Knead for 8 minutes by hand or for 5 minutes in the mixer. Add the dried fruit and mixed peel and knead for another 2 minutes to mix them in.

Put the dough into the prepared loaf pan, cover with a light kitchen towel or napkin and leave to rise in a warm place (by a radiator, for instance, or a sunny window) for 1 hour, or until doubled in size.

Meanwhile, preheat the oven to 350°F (180°C/Gas mark 4).

Remove the covering and bake for 45 minutes, or until deep golden brown on top. When you think the loaf is ready, gently loosen the sides with a spatula and tip it out of the pan. If it's fully cooked, it should sound slightly hollow when you tap it on the bottom and feel springy when you lightly squeeze the sides. Place it on a wire rack to cool.

Slice up the loaf and serve either fresh or toasted, and buttered.

Chocolate, raisin, and almond cookies

Vegetarian

Makes 16 to 18

Preparation time: 15 minutes

Cooking time: 10 minutes

Ready in 35 minutes

⅔ cup (150g) butter

1¼ cups (150g) all-purpose (plain) flour

½ teaspoon baking soda (bicarbonate of soda)

½ cup (50g) ground almonds

½ cup (50g) steel-cut oats (stone or porridge oats)

⅓ cup (50g) raisins

¼ cup packed (50g) brown sugar

4 tablespoons (50g) superfine (caster) or granulated sugar

3½ ounces (100g) dark chocolate, cut into chunks, or ½ cup chocolate chips

1 large egg yolk or 2 small ones

The oats in these cookies give them a wonderful and ever so slightly chewy texture. The ground almonds make them moist, and the slight bitterness of the dark chocolate is offset by the sweetness of the sugar and raisins. These are refined enough to serve after dinner with coffee, but I don't need an excuse to eat two or three!

Preheat the oven to 350°F (180°C/Gas mark 4).

Melt the butter in a saucepan over medium heat. Remove from the heat and set aside to cool.

Sift the flour and baking soda into a bowl, then stir in the ground almonds, oats, raisins, brown sugar, superfine or granulated sugar, and chocolate.

Mix the egg yolk with the cooled melted butter. Add to the dry ingredients and stir to mix everything together. Use your hands to make walnut-size balls and arrange slightly apart from each other on two baking sheets. Gently flatten slightly.

Bake for 8 to 10 minutes, until golden. Allow to cool for a few minutes, then use a metal spatula or palette knife to transfer them to a wire rack to cool completely.

Ginger cookies

Vegetarian

Makes about 50

Preparation time: 10 minutes

Cooking time: 15 minutes

Ready in 35 minutes

1 cup (225g) butter, softened

1 cup (225g) superfine (caster) or granulated sugar

½ cup (150g) golden syrup (or substitute dark corn syrup)

1 egg

3½ cups (450g) all-purpose (plain) flour

1 tablespoon ground ginger

1 teaspoon baking soda (bicarbonate of soda), sifted

These cookies were my dad's favorites, so they were one of the first things I baked when I was younger. This recipe makes quite a lot, but you can freeze the unbaked cookies and cook from frozen. They'll take 5 to 10 minutes longer.

Preheat the oven to 350°F (180°C/Gas mark 4).

Combine all the ingredients in a food processor and pulse a few times until they come together to form a soft dough. If you don't have a food processor, cream the butter in a bowl, then add in the sugar and golden syrup and beat together. Then stir in the rest of the ingredients to form a soft dough.

Use your hands to form walnut-size balls of the dough and place them a couple of inches (6cm) apart on a baking sheet (no need to grease it). You will need two or three baking sheets, or you can make them in two or three batches.

Bake for 10 to 15 minutes, or until golden brown. Remove the baking sheets from the oven and allow to cool for a few minutes, then use a metal spatula or palette knife to remove them to a wire rack to cool.

Shortbread

Vegetarian

Makes 25

Preparation time: 15 minutes

Cooking time: 10 minutes

Ready in 35 minutes

1¼ cups (150g) all-purpose (plain) flour

4 tablespoons (50g) superfine (caster) or granulated sugar

7 tablespoons (100g) butter, softened

This shortbread is quick to make, crisp and buttery, and wonderfully versatile. It is a great go-to recipe to serve plain, with tea or coffee, or with desserts such as Fluffy Lemon Pudding (page 178) and Carrageen Moss Pudding (page 197).

Preheat the oven to 350°F (180°C/Gas mark 4).

Combine the flour and sugar in a mixing bowl. Rub in the butter and bring the whole mixture together to form a stiff dough. Do not add any water.

Roll out the dough to a thickness of about ¼ inch (5mm) and cut into shapes. Place carefully on a baking sheet about 1 inch (3cm) apart.

Bake for 6 to 10 minutes, or until pale golden. Using a spatula, carefully transfer the shortbread onto a wire rack to cool.

Variations
Add 1 teaspoon ground ginger, or 1 teaspoon ground cinnamon, or finely grated zest of 1 orange, or finely grated zest of 1 lemon, or 2 tablespoons sifted cocoa powder, or 2 teaspoons dried lavender.

Whole-grain shortbread

Vegetarian

Makes about 20

Preparation time: 15 minutes

Cooking time: 10 minutes

Ready in 35 minutes

⅔ cup (75g) whole wheat (wholemeal) flour

9 tablespoons (75g) all-purpose (plain) flour

1 cup (100g) butter, softened

4 tablespoons (50g) superfine (caster) or granulated sugar

My boys love making these as they can choose whatever shapes they like. They are great for birthday parties and lunch boxes. They are also good sandwiched together with raspberry jam!

Preheat the oven to 350°F (180°C/Gas mark 4).

Combine all of the ingredients in a food processor and whiz until the mixture almost comes together and resembles coarse bread crumbs. Tip onto the work surface and bring it together with your hands. If you are not using a food processor, rub the butter into the combined flour and sugar in a bowl and bring together with your hands.

Sprinkle your work surface with a little flour (whole wheat or white) and roll out the dough to a thickness of about ¼ inch (5mm) or roll it between two pieces of plastic wrap (cling film). Using a cookie cutter, cut into whatever shapes you wish or just cut simply into squares with a knife. Transfer to a baking sheet (no need to grease or line it) spaced about 1 inch (3cm) apart.

Bake for 6 to 10 minutes depending on the size, until they are pale golden and feel firm on top. Using a spatula, remove carefully and cool on a wire rack.

Oaty shortbread

Vegetarian

Makes about 40

Preparation time: 15 minutes

Cooking time: 20 minutes

Ready in 45 minutes

1¾ cups (275g) rolled oats

¾ cup (100g) all-purpose (plain) flour

¾ cup (150g) superfine (caster) or granulated sugar

½ teaspoon baking soda (bicarbonate of soda)

1 teaspoon salt

1 cup (225g) butter, softened

These lovely cookies are surprisingly delicate even though they contain hearty oats. My children love them, and I often put them in their school lunch boxes—though sweet, the addition of oats makes them good and nutritious (just don't tell them!).

Preheat the oven to 350°F (180°C/Gas mark 4).

Whiz the oats in a food processor until they are quite fine. Then add the remaining ingredients and whiz again until the dough comes together.

Roll out the dough on a floured work surface to a thickness of about ¼ inch (5mm). Cut into squares, circles, or shapes with cookie cutters and place on baking sheets (no need to grease or line) spaced about 1 inch (3cm) apart.

Bake for 15 to 20 minutes, until pale golden and slightly firm. Using a spatula, carefully transfer to a wire rack to cool. These will keep for 5 to 6 days in an airtight container, and they freeze well, too.

Oatcakes

Vegetarian

Makes about 30

Preparation time: 15 minutes

Cooking time: 20 minutes

Ready in 45 minutes

1¼ cups (200g) rolled oats

¼ teaspoon salt

¼ teaspoon baking powder

2 tablespoons (25g) butter, softened

1 tablespoon extra virgin olive oil

½ cup (100ml) boiling water

A handful of finely ground oatmeal, for rolling

Mixed seeds, such as sesame, millet, poppy, or golden flaxseeds (linseeds), freshly ground black pepper or salt crystals, such as Maldon, for sprinkling (optional)

Oatcakes are perfect for anyone with wheat intolerance. Few things rival them for serving with cheese. They aren't strongly flavored— some people put spices in their oatcakes but I don't think that's necessary. The oatcakes should only play a supporting role while the cheese itself is the star of the show.

Preheat the oven 325°F (170°C/Gas mark 3).

Combine the oats, salt, and baking powder in a food processor and whiz for 2 minutes until it is finer in texture and looks similar to ground almonds. Add the butter and whiz until combined.

With the motor running, pour in the olive oil and boiling water, stopping frequently to check if the dough is coming together. Don't let it get too wet.

Turn the dough out onto a work surface dusted with finely ground oats and knead just to bring it together. Roll the dough out as thinly as possible, to a thickness of ¹⁄₁₆ to ⅛ inch (2–3mm). Sprinkle the dough with seeds or grind some pepper or sprinkle some salt on top, if you wish. Give the dough another light roll to make sure the seeds stay on.

Using a 2- to 3¼-inch (5–8mm) round cutter or a knife, cut the dough into rounds, triangles, or squares. You can re-roll and use the scraps as well. Place on baking sheets (don't oil or butter) spaced about 1½ inches (4cm) apart.

Bake for 15 to 20 minutes, until lightly browned on the edges and crisp. Transfer to a wire rack to cool.

Whole-grain sesame seed cheese crackers

Vegetarian

Makes 25 to 30

Preparation time: 10 minutes

Cooking time: 45 minutes

Ready in 1 hour 10 minutes

- ¾ cup (100g) whole wheat (wholemeal) flour
- ¾ cup (100g) all-purpose (plain) flour, plus extra for dusting work top
- 3 tablespoons sesame seeds
- ¾ teaspoon salt
- ½ teaspoon baking powder
- 2 tablespoons (25g) butter
- 1 tablespoon light (single) cream
- 4 to 5 tablespoons water

These nutritious crackers are full of wholesome seeds as well as whole wheat. They have a lovely sesame flavor that works best with strongly flavored cheeses.

Preheat the oven to 300°F (150°C/Gas mark 2). Lightly flour a baking sheet.

In a bowl, mix together the flours, sesame seeds, salt, and baking powder. Rub in the butter and cream until the mixture resembles loose bread crumbs. Add just enough water to form a firm dough.

Dust a work top and the dough with flour. Roll out the dough to a thickness of about ¹⁄₁₆ or ⅛ inch (about 2mm). Prick all over with a fork, then cut into rounds measuring about 2⅜ inches (6cm) in diameter using a cookie cutter. Or cut into squares using a knife or pastry wheel. Transfer to the prepared baking sheet spaced about 2 inches (5cm) apart.

Bake for about 45 minutes, or until lightly browned and quite crisp. Remove from the oven and transfer to a wire rack to cool.

Index

This edition first published in 2013 by Collins.

This book includes recipes and images first published in *Rachel's Favourite Food at Home* (2006), *Rachel's Food for Living* (2007), *Rachel's Diary 2009* (2008), *Bake* (2008), *Home Cooking* (2009), *Entertaining at Home* (2010), *Easy Meals* (2011) and *Cake* (2012).

HarperCollins*Publishers*
77–85 Fulham Palace Road
London W6 8JB

www.harpercollins.co.uk
www.harpercollins.com

10 9 8 7 6 5 4 3 2 1

Photography © Christian Barnett 2006, Peter Cassidy 2006, Georgia Glynn Smith 2007, Mark Read 2008, Noel Murphy 2008, David Loftus 2009, Kate Whitaker 2010, Philip Webb, 2011, 2012, Lis Parsons 2013.

Picture credits © p53 Felix Zaska/Corbis (top), Christophe Boisvieux/Corbis (bottom left), Getty Images (bottom right); p93 Paul A. Souders/Corbis (top left), Hubert Stadler/Corbis (top right), Ocean/Corbis (bottom); p141 Jonathan Andrew/Corbis (top), Charlie Mahoney/Corbis (bottom left), National Geographic/Getty Images (bottom right); p187 Bertrand Rieger/Hemis/Corbis (top), Michael S. Yamashita/Corbis (bottom left), */Design Pics/Corbis (bottom right).

A catalogue record for this book is available from the British Library.

ISBN: 978-0-00-746258-2

Printed and bound in China by South China Printing Co Ltd.

Collins